ISBN# 978-1-60461-559-3

Cover design by Loveseat Creative
www.loveseatcreative.com
Photos used by permission

World-Changers: LIVE TO SERVE

By Walt Kallestad
& Bob Beltz

"It is never easy to be a world-changer; they are often misunderstood in their generation. They go beyond conventional wisdom and follow the voice of God and their conscience. This book powerfully illustrates these truths and calls each of us to bold steps of obedience and perseverance.

The romance of life is not in the length of days lived, but in our steps of obedience that glorify God and make us all world-changers."

Don Leetch and Dean Kerns
Founders, DaySpring Greeting Cards

To Phil Anschutz,
A modern-day world-changer

Table of Contents

Foreword

As I sat and watched the movie *Amazing Grace*, I was captivated by the story of one individual with a passion to do what was right, in spite of a society that accepted injustice as a way of life, and in spite of repeated setbacks and disappointments. It is a powerful story of commitment, bravery, courage, and persistence. It is a story of the journey of one totally dedicated person making a significant difference in the world.

William Wilberforce struggled with whether, as a Christian, he could serve his Lord effectively in a secular job, or if he had to be in the ministry to live out his Christian faith. Through the encouragement of friends, he came to realize that we are all called to serve God no matter who we are, where we live, or what our occupation. His life is a testimony to living out our faith in the workplace today.

In the process, he had to change the minds and hearts of people that would cause a whole society to open up their eyes to both truth and injustice. As I left the theater that evening, I was inspired to be more of a difference-maker in my corner of the world.

You may say, "I am not William Wilberforce. He was a unique individual." But remember that he was a human being just like you and me. He had the same doubts, the same sense of inadequacy, and the same fears, but he was driven by a purpose in life that was greater than himself. In many respects he was an ordinary person who cared more about others than he cared about himself; what a wonderful legacy he has left for us.

Have you ever stopped to ask yourself what is your purpose in life? What are you really passionate about? You may feel very ordinary, but I have seen ordinary people accomplish the extraordinary, even the impossible—far more than they ever dreamed or thought they could. Making a difference is what the Christian life is all about.

How do I do that in my life? That's what this book does so well—it is a practical application of the principles of a world-changer that can be effectively applied in any life today. I believe you will find this book will inspire you to a deeper sense of commitment to being a world-changer and to accomplish all that God has prepared you for.

William Wilberforce did not do what he did as a lesson for us. He did it because he was following a higher calling, and in the process he has provided an exciting inspiration to us and a path that we can choose to follow. Let me encourage you to investigate that path.

—Don Soderquist,
Retired COO and Vice Chairman,
Wal-Mart Stores, Inc.

Acknowledgments

We would like to give special thanks to a few people that made this book a reality. First, we could not have made this happen without Patrick Kallestad (Walt's son and Bob's friend). Thanks for quarterbacking the project!

Tom Winters and Jeff Dunn were our agents on the project and really helped pull all the pieces together to get the book done. Chris Robinette, Kelly Nichols, and Jeremy Ennis went the extra mile to accomplish the publication of the book in "Guinness Book of Record" speed. Thank you Adam Palmer for taking our scattered thoughts and putting them down on paper—or binary code.

We are very grateful to Don Soderquist for believing enough in the entire World-Changer enterprise to encourage us and to write the Foreword.

Finally, you have heard it said that behind every successful man you will find a surprised mother-in-law. But the truth is, behind all our efforts in life and ministry we have two of the greatest women on the planet cheering us on: our wives!

Thanks Ali. Thanks Mary.

—*Walt & Bob*

CHAPTER ONE:
Who in the World is William Wilberforce?

I (Bob) don't really have an official title. The people who have titles came up with the term "Without Portfolio" to refer to us non-titled types. What I do is serve as an advisor for The Anschutz Corporation of Denver, Colorado. The Anschutz Corporation owns the filmmaking company Walden Media, and as an advisor, I do what I can to make sure our films live up the overall vision and mission of our company. So when my boss said he wanted to do a film about the life of William Wilberforce, I was ecstatic. Walden and its sister company Bristol Bay Productions have been given the mission of making family-friendly movies that are uplifting, inspiring, and encouraging; movies that can be seen by the entire family without parents being embarrassed that their children are being exposed to vulgarity, immorality, and violence. The story of Wilberforce certainly lives up to that standard.

But beyond that, I knew that the story of William Wilberforce had the power to change people's lives. It wasn't just a nice story, or an uplifting story, or a heartwarming story—Wilberforce had such a monumental impact on history, I knew that, if we did the movie right, we could send people out of the theatre truly inspired.

And that became the film *Amazing Grace.*

But before the movie, there was a man. An ordinary, wild-haired, sickly, not-exactly-handsome man who was a member of the British Parliament. And this ordinary man stood on the floor of that Parliament one day and, after years and years of work, brought down the biggest giant England had ever seen: the slave trade.

Who was William Wilberforce, you ask? I asked the same question once. I was a pastor who decided to dig into the life of this regular guy to examine his impact on history. And the more I dug, the more I saw parallels between Wilberforce and our modern times.

Two hundred years, to the day, before our movie *Amazing Grace* released in theatres, William Wilberforce won an almost twenty-year battle against the slave trade in England. It's impressive on its own, but let's put this in perspective, relative to our world today. Slavery back then wasn't just an accepted form of labor—it was an enormous economic force throughout the British Empire. So many people were making so much money on the sale of forced human labor that the slave trade was, essentially, the cornerstone of the English economy.

A good equivalent for today would be this: imagine leading a crusade, on your own, in Washington, D.C., to shut down the top one hundred corporations in America. Amazon.com, Coca-Cola, GM, Google—all the big ones, shut down for good.

That's what William Wilberforce did.

And he did it because of a grand conviction that slavery in itself was wrong. He was the man who popularized the truth that slaves are human beings, and therefore should not be oppressed through slavery. Oddly enough, this was a new idea in England in the late 1700s. We've come a long way since then, haven't we?

And we have Wilberforce to thank for it.

The man was, simply put, a world-changer.

But he was just one man, and he lived two hundred years ago. Plus, people like him are one in a million. And what he did was *so* extravagant, *so* enormous—there's no way anyone alive today can change the world the way he did. Right?

Not so fast.

As I lived with Wilberforce's story while developing *Amazing Grace*, I kept asking the question: what was it about this man? What did he have in his life that allowed him to do this? Was he an anomaly, or can we use some of the same tools he did and change our own world?

So I started to take apart Wilberforce's life and look deeply into it, and I found seven principles, seven character traits Wilberforce possessed that are available to us today. There are many parallels between his life and ours. Between the actions he took and the actions we can take. Between the disciplines he enacted and the disciplines we can enact.

And so that's what we're going to do in this book. We're going to examine the life of this extraordinarily ordinary man to uncover some truths about him, and in so doing, we just may uncover a few truths about ourselves.

Wilberforce and the Mount

There was another man who was a world-changer. A man who preceded William Wilberforce by about eighteen hundred years. A man who had such an impact on history that historians picked his birth to be the pivot, the shift, of the way we *record* history.

Of course, I mean Jesus of Nazareth.

As a pastor, I (Walt) have had the privilege of studying the life and words of Jesus as part of my call for years. And the thing I love the most about it is that it never gets old. His words are so deep and rich that, though I have so many of them memorized, they still hold truth, power, and discovery.

Some of Jesus' most famous words come from what we call the Sermon on the Mount, found recorded in the gospel of Matthew. From chapter five through chapter seven, Jesus never stops talking, and each word we read drips with the wisdom of God Himself. I find myself hanging on every syllable, eager to find something new within those familiar phrases, and often doing just that.

It's amazing how well the Sermon on the Mount lines up with the life of William Wilberforce, almost as if the life of the British politician was based on this historical and world-changing treatise on blessings, the Law of Moses, murder, adultery, divorce, enemies, the poor, prayer, fasting, heavenly treasures, earthly treasures, anxiety, superiority complexes, heavenly gifts, narrow and wide gates, trees, fruit, foolishness, and wisdom.

It's deep, and it isn't for the faint of heart. Jesus dared to speak controversial things, just like Wilberforce would do later in history. He tackled the status quo and set some people straight, correcting a lot of half-truths and complete falsehoods they'd believed.

In addition to the Sermon on the Mount, Jesus spoke some strong words to his disciples about changing the world, words we find in the gospel of Matthew:

"...Go and make disciples of all the nations, baptizing them in the name of the Father and the Son and the Holy Spirit. Teach these new disciples to obey all the commands I have given you. And be sure of this: I am with you always, even to the end of the age." (Matthew 28:19-20, NLT)

Christians have historically looked at that passage of scripture and treated it as a call to evangelism, as a command to take the story of Jesus into the world around us. And it is that, unequivocally. But something else is there, underneath the surface, an implied encouragement that applies to every one of us.

Because with those words, Jesus was telling his disciples—and if you subscribe to his teachings, you are one of them—that they were world-changers. To take it a step farther, there's not a person alive who *can't* be a world-changer.

It's been estimated that less than 1% of the population of our planet shapes the circumstances, experiences, and culture of the other 99%. That is staggering proof that, indeed, there are very few world-changers *acting* today.

But how many world-changers have been lulled into inactivity?

How many world-changers are sitting at home today doing nothing, and as a result are completely unhappy in their lives?

How many world-changers are paying closer attention to their favorite sports team, or the latest blockbuster movie, or an internet chat room, or any of the thousands of other things in this world that can occupy our time than to the needs of the world around them?

I believe each of us has the ability to be a world-changer. Wilberforce was a special man, but he isn't the only person ever to change the world. Jesus did it, and he said we can do it, too.

Along the way of studying Wilberforce's life, we're going to unpack Jesus' richly layered Sermon on the Mount to find how the words of Jesus line up with the life of our featured world-changer. I am confident we'll be more than a little surprised at what we find.

But I advise caution: once you read this book, you may wind up being a world-changer yourself. Accept the consequences if you dare. You've been warned.

It's All Ancient History

Probably the crucial question when speaking of both Wilberforce and Jesus is this: Isn't it all just ancient history? There's no one really doing any of that sort of thing today, is there?

Honestly, there is. As we explore the life of Wilberforce and the words of Jesus, we're going to offer a few stories from our lives and the lives of those we know to show you that world-changing moments are happening almost every day, in the here and now. They're happening in our lives, they're happening in our nation, they're happening around the world.

In fact, they're probably happening around you. You just aren't aware of it yet.

They've happened in recent history, and they'll happen in the near future.

They've been happening since the beginning of time, and they'll happen until time stops.

World-changing moments are always lurking around the corner, waiting for an opportunity to pounce. We're going to share a very few examples of people who've let those moments tackle them, and who seized them right back.

People who have changed the world.

People like Wilberforce. People like us.

People like you.

Let's get started.

CHAPTER TWO:
Pardon

William Wilberforce did not set out to change the world. When he entered Parliament at the age of 21, he was not intent on bringing about social justice through legislation. He was not rested and ready for the nearly twenty-year fight that lay ahead. He had not whipped himself into a frenzy like a linebacker just before the snap of the ball, intent on dropping the quarterback for a loss.

Do you know what Wilberforce was interested in when he entered Parliament? Playing cards. Socializing with the upper crust members of society. Getting in good with the "right" people so he could live out the rest of his life in comfort, snug in the warm blanket of politics.

Wilberforce was all about himself.

His parents were wealthy, merchant class people, so he was considered a gentleman, a man of high standing in society. Someone of status. All signs in his life pointed to taking it easy for the next sixty years or so. Days in Parliament arguing eloquently with his fellow Ministers, evenings with one of his many card-playing associates, sipping brandy in a parlor or pub somewhere. Parties and socials and cricket on the lawn.

But it hadn't always been like that. As a young man, Wilberforce was deeply influenced by a man named John

Newton, a man who became his spiritual mentor of sorts. Wilberforce's father died when William was quite young, and his mother sent him to live with his Aunt and Uncle. John Newton was one of their spiritual mentors and began to have an influence on their nephew, and as a young boy, William came to faith in Christ. But when he began to write letters home about his newfound faith to his mother, she became concerned that he was becoming a religious fanatic and brought him home to get him away from Newton. It would be nearly twenty years until the two met again, and by the time William became a student at Cambridge University, he had lost his childhood faith.

Newton himself was a former slave trader who threw himself upon God's mercy when a slave ship he was aboard began to sink. He converted to Christianity but still, astonishingly, continued in the slave trade, personally overseeing the transport of more than 20,000 slaves from Africa to the West Indies. Fortunately for him, for the slaves, and for Wilberforce, God reached into Newton's life and, over time, worked on his heart to convince him that the slave trade was wrong. If you can believe it, back then, one could still be a Christian and a trader of slaves. The two things were not seen as anachronistic or hypocritical.

This was the prevailing mindset of Wilberforce's time: that slaves weren't really humans. They were property. It was the mindset Newton had for a long time, but that God eventually broke him of, causing him to realize his own depravity and need for grace. It was this realization that led him to write the line "saved a wretch like me" in his famous hymn "Amazing Grace."

Another tutor and mentor Wilberforce had was a man named Isaac Milner, a brilliant mathematician who held the Newtonian Chair at Cambridge (that's "Newtonian" as in "Isaac Newton," the first man to mathematically describe the effects of gravity). Milner not only had an influence on Wilberforce's intellect, but as a deep Christian who held his faith close to his vest, he had a profound influence on Wilberforce's spirituality, though it would be revealed later in his life.

Upon graduation, Wilberforce entered politics straight-away, and he was welcomed into Parliament (the British law-making body) at the age of 21. He was joined in Parliament by his best friend, William Pitt, who would become England's youngest Prime Minister at the age of 23. Pitt would later become a huge ally to Wilberforce, but at this time in their lives, the men were content simply to lounge around together and enjoy the life of high society and all it had to offer.

In October of 1784, Wilberforce took a vacation with his mother and sister to the French Riviera, and, deciding he didn't want to be the only man stuck with two women on the very long trip, he invited his old tutor Isaac Milner to join them. The men bonded while away on vacation, though Wilberforce had no idea that Milner was a firm Christian.

One fateful day, when the conversation turned to a particular British clergyman whom Wilberforce deemed to be a bit too enthusiastic in his evangelistic pursuits, Milner took umbrage at the comment and revealed his faith to his young pupil, who was astonished that deep faith and steep intellect could coexist in one man.

The two began to talk extensively about God. Wilberforce's sister had brought along a book by Philip Doddridge with the tantalizing title *The Rise and Progress of Religion and the Soul*, so Wilberforce and Milner decided it would be a perfect time to study the book together, as well as the scriptures of the Bible.

And thus the wheels of faith began to turn in Wilberforce's head once more. Unlike many people, Wilberforce didn't have a flash conversion to Christianity—his was a gradual turning, like a great ocean liner correcting its course over time.

When Wilberforce returned home to England, he sought out his old friend and mentor John Newton to quiz him about this concept of Christianity as a lifestyle. He wanted to dig deeper into his new faith beliefs, and Newton helped him do just that. And as Wilberforce turned his heart more and more toward God, he finally experienced what he later described in his prayer journal as his "Great Change."

This great change became the foundation, the bedrock for his faith in Christ, and it left him with a great question: what do I do now? The trajectory of his life to that point had been pointing toward politics, even to the point of spending wild amounts of money to ensure he had enough votes to sustain his position. But he now had such an abiding love for God that he didn't know how he could remain in political office. His life was at a crossroads.

Wilberforce had experienced Pardon. The "Great Change" he described in his prayer journal was a pardon, offered to him by God. Newton wrote about Pardon in "Amazing Grace." Milner described Pardon to Wilberforce on their trip. Every person who has ever embraced the person of Jesus has accepted Pardon. It is the door through which we walk into changing the world.

Pardon is a way of looking past our moral failures, our innate, human flaws, and moving on with our lives with vigor and direction. It is the spark that ignites us and starts us on the road to becoming a world-changer.

Pardon on the Mount

Wilberforce experienced a sort of crisis of conscience when he fully converted to the Christian faith. He felt he had to give up his societal life in order to truly live out his beliefs, that his faith ran cross-grain to his current lifestyle. The teachings of Jesus, in Wilberforce's estimation, were completely against the current of the culture of the time, and he didn't know what to do with it.

Jesus also espoused some counter-cultural beliefs, talking about this principle of Pardon in his Sermon on the Mount, though in a completely different context. In Matthew 5, we read:

"So if you are presenting a sacrifice at the altar in the Temple and you suddenly remember that someone has something against you, leave your sacrifice there at the altar. Go and be reconciled to that person. Then come and offer your sacrifice to God." (Matthew 5:23-24, NLT)

A handful of verses later, Jesus spends two full paragraphs deflating the normal, human idea of revenge:

"You have heard the law that says the punishment must match the injury: 'An eye for an eye, and a tooth for a tooth.' But I say, do not resist an evil person! If someone slaps you on the right cheek, offer the other cheek also. If you are sued in court and your shirt is taken from you, give your coat, too. If a soldier demands that you carry his gear for a mile, carry it two miles. Give to those who ask, and don't turn away from those who want to borrow.

"You have heard the law that says, 'Love your neighbor' and hate your enemy. But I say, love your enemies! Pray for those who persecute you! In that way, you will be acting as true children of your Father in heaven. For he gives his sunlight to both the evil and the good, and he sends rain on the just and the unjust alike. If you love only those who love you, what reward is there for that? Even corrupt tax collectors do that much. If you are kind only to your friends, how are you different from anyone else? Even pagans do that. But you are to be perfect, even as your Father in heaven is perfect." (Matthew 5:38-48, NLT)

In this instance, Pardon isn't just something we receive from God—it's something we offer to other people.

Even worse, it's about pardoning people who don't deserve it.

Why would Jesus condemn us to such a lifestyle of depressing piety? Does he just want us to be a bunch of doormats who let the world walk all over us? Or is he hoping to raise an army of one goody-two-shoes after another so we can kill the enemy with kindness?

Or is it possible that Jesus is teaching us something completely different?

Look at the examples he uses in verses 38-42. If someone slaps you on one cheek, let them slap you on the other. If someone takes your coat from you in court, give them your shirt, too. Don't just put up with a demand to shoulder a burden—put in extra effort and carry it farther.

All of these instances, if they happened to us, would probably cause us to stamp our collective feet, clench our collective fists, and let out a collective, "But it's not *fair*!" Jesus is really pushing our buttons with these examples—in each of them, something completely unfair happens in the first place, and he says not only *not* to put up a fuss, but also to let them get away with *more* than they did originally.

Why? What's his point?

Why would he then continue, in verses 43-48, to tell us that we have to love our enemies? That we have to be kind to them? He really twists the knife, too, in verses 46 and 47, pointing out that even ungodly and corrupt people can be nice to someone who's already being nice.

Again: what's the point?

Maybe—just maybe—Jesus is showing us how *he* feels. We've all messed up, we've all made mistakes, some of us seemingly more than others, but not a one of us is perfect.

The good thing about Jesus is that, through his life on earth, death on the cross, and resurrection back to life, we can have those past mistakes erased. We can be Pardoned for them.

But not all of us choose Pardon. Some of us choose to wallow in our mistakes, to keep doing wrong, to choose our own selfishness over Christ's sacrifice. And when we do that? We slap him on the cheek.

But Jesus being Jesus, he shows us the other cheek. His offer of Pardon still stands, no matter how many times we resist or refuse it.

Because Jesus knows that Pardon is that first step toward changing the world. He knows it is impossible for us to change the world without first being changed ourselves. That's where it all begins. That's where it began for Wilberforce, and that's where it begins for us.

But what about verses 23-24, where Jesus talks about

all this "presenting an offer at the altar in the Temple" and that sort of thing? We don't even mess with offerings at the Temple anymore—how does that apply to us? And why the altar imagery? What in the world does that have to do with Pardon?

It has everything to do with it. Because God wants us to walk with Pardoning hearts. And you know what? It's so important to him that he'll take a breather while you take care of it. You could be on the cusp of communicating with him, at the very edge of meeting him face to face, and he still thinks Pardon is more important. He isn't demanding at all, saying, "Your sacrifice is on the altar *now*! You *must* offer it or I won't accept it! I'm *God*, for crying out loud! Thou shalt not keep me waiting!"

No. He says, "I'm more concerned with your heart and your relationships with my other children. Take care of that *immediately*. Don't wait. There is no time to lose."

We must Pardon others, and we must receive Pardon for ourselves. This is where true world-changing begins.

Pardon in the Real World: Bob

I (Bob) have a story similar to William Wilberforce's, though instead of having a realization of God while on vacation with a math genius, I had my realization on a football field as holy hell broke loose around me.

Let me back up. I had absolutely no spiritual background growing up. My family wasn't religious at all; we spent Sundays just like every other day. As a consequence, I grew up to become a very tough individual who made many, many, mistakes on my way to adulthood.

I eventually got to the point where I figured I was beyond hope. That even if there was a God, and even if he did have arms longer than the Mississippi River, he wouldn't be able to reach far enough down to pick me up. That's how distressed I was.

By the time I got to college, I was hardened to the idea of God. I once had a professor who shared my hardness, and I used to quote him when people would try to talk to me about Jesus: "Look, if Jesus existed," I would say, "he was nothing more than an insignificant person in history." Then, over their sputters of protest, I would continue: "And if God exists," I would say, "he doesn't care."

I was convinced I couldn't live the Christian life, not with all my hardness and toughness and rough past. I couldn't do all that "turn the other cheek" stuff—if someone slapped my cheek, I was going to deck them.

But when I was twenty years old, I wound up hanging out with some Christian guys, and they began to talk to me about a relationship with Christ. It was very subtle, very gentle, not preachy at all. But as I watched them and the way they lived their lives, I began to get a sense that I'd been wrong about Christianity—that it was more about a relationship with the person of Jesus than it was about following all the tenets of a dry and stuffy religion.

One time these new friends invited me to play in

a football game—for their inter-church league. One church's team versus another church's team, just out to have some fun and healthy competition.

As these things tend to go, the longer the game progressed, the more intense the play became. It's just one of those things that happens, some instinctive, militaristic fight-or-flight response that kicks in when you're in the midst of athletic competition. One of the players on our team used to be a middle linebacker for the Kansas City Chiefs, and during one play, someone on the other team gave him a forearm to the nose, which started a gusher of blood emanating from his nostrils.

It was probably an accident. Maybe not. Regardless, at the end of the next play, the man who'd given that forearm was lying flat on his back, unconscious at the hand of our NFL retiree middle linebacker.

And then the fight began.

Right there in the middle of the heavenly Christian brotherhood, all hell broke loose. The two teams turned on each other, and it became a genuine fray. Fists were flying everywhere, strong language was flying right along with it, and mixed in were dirt, grass, and bits of clothing (and possibly teeth or hair).

And I stood in the middle of it, completely detached, watching this brawl as it went down. And that's when I had the realization: *I can be a Christian!*

It suddenly made sense to me. These guys weren't perfect people—far from it. They were just regular guys from all walks of life and all backgrounds temporarily giving in to their humanity. They were a bunch of forgiven sinners.

They seemed to be a lot like me. I had the "sin" part down; I just needed to get a handle on the "forgiven" part.

Even so, I didn't fall on my knees right there on the field and start confessing all my sins among the pummeled. The fight broke up, we finished the game, said our apologies where necessary, and I went home.

Shortly after that, one of my imperfect Christian friends told me I should read the Gospel of John. I took him up on the challenge, and by the time I got to the third chapter, I had a "Great Change" moment similar to Wilberforce's. It was like God found a light switch inside my soul and flipped it on. Suddenly, I realized that what I was reading was completely true, and I had a decision to make:

Act on that truth? Or ignore it?

It was, quite honestly, one of the easiest decisions I've ever made. If Jesus was real, and was going to give me the ability to live a better life, wouldn't I be an idiot not to accept it?

I gave in to Pardon. To this day, it remains the best decision I ever made.

Pardon in the Real World: Walt

I (Walt) gave in to Pardon when I accepted Christ very

early in life, but that wasn't the only time I did it. Pardon is something we have to accept continually, a truth I learned in 2002 when I experienced a massive heart attack.

You've heard of "quadruple-bypass" surgery? Usually when doctors say that, they say it in hushed tones, with great reverence—it's a major procedure. My heart attack required even more. Technically, my surgery was "sextuple-bypass" surgery. Six bypasses. Six.

As you can imagine, I was very ill. But I was determined to get better, so I decided it was up to me to take control of my healing. I was a well-known, well-respected pastor of a large church; how would it look for me to suffer from an illness like this? Wasn't I supposed to be strong and courageous instead of weak and needy? Wasn't I supposed to be a light for others to look at?

I was determined to get better, so I called every doctor I needed to and got information on every possible medication out there. I searched out the best exercises to perform. I did exhaustive research to find the most heart-healthy diet I could eat. Now there's nothing wrong with becoming better-informed; but being informed doesn't mean being in charge. If I'm in charge, God isn't.

And nine months later, I still wasn't better.

After all this work, all this initial striving toward making myself better, I hadn't moved an inch toward health.

I was trying to do it myself, trying to make it all better under my own power. I hadn't yet accepted Pardon from

God.

So I got on my knees and asked him to forgive me for my foolishness. I asked for Pardon. "God," I said, "I'm sorry for trying to control my healing. I give this all to you." And in that moment, I began to hear the song "I Surrender All" with my spiritual ears. And then God spoke four cherished words to my quite literally broken heart: "I have healed you."

I've been better ever since.

Pardon was the first step toward my healing. I tried to change my own world, and my body betrayed me. I got myself out of the way, accepted God's Pardon, and suddenly I was whole.

It all began with Pardon.

But it doesn't end there.

CHAPTER THREE:
Purpose

William Wilberforce's "Great Change" affected him deeply and caused him to question his career path. That acceptance of Pardon started a quest to find something else, the next step in his world-changing life: Purpose.

At this point in his life, Wilberforce began to feel a deep sense of something Christians like to label "God's calling." The Bible is rich with the metaphor that God has called his people to a specific task, and Wilberforce felt that calling heavily. His immediate response was to reexamine his political aspirations.

In his day, there was no question about what he should do. When people had those "Great Change" types of experiences, they went to seminary and became clergymen. In our modern terminology, he would've become a preacher or the pastor of a church. And that's what he thought he should do.

But Wilberforce struggled with the notion that he *had* to leave Parliament. He wanted to serve God, to be sure, but he wasn't sure that entering the full-time ministry was necessarily the way to do it. He had to determine if it was even *possible* to serve God in his existing career, even though he quietly feared that he would be expected to devote his life to full-time ministry.

So he went to see his old friend John Newton and put the question to him: which would God rather me do—serve him in ministry or serve in Parliament? Newton's answer is marvelously portrayed in the film *Amazing Grace*, where he says something along the lines of, "Perhaps God has placed you in politics to do something there." The idea that God could use him in politics both thrilled and flummoxed Wilberforce, perhaps because he dared not dream that he could unite the two worlds.

Still seeking an answer, Wilberforce wrote to his good friend William Pitt, who had now become Prime Minister. Pitt was not a Christian, not even really a believer in God, but his answer, like Newton's, surprised Wilberforce: "Surely the principles of Christianity lead to action as well as meditation."

There is a marvelous scene in *Amazing Grace* where a group of Christian abolitionists have come to dinner at Wilberforce's home to convince him to join the abolition movement. At a point in time, one of the abolitionists named Thomas Clarkson says to Wilberforce, "We understand you are having trouble deciding whether to do the work of God, or of a political activist." Then Hannah More, one of the great literary figures of Wilberforce's time says, "May we suggest... you can do both."

The combination of counsel from his spiritual mentor and from his best friend and peers—all of whom told him the same thing: that he could serve God in the political realm—convinced Wilberforce that he was to stay in his post in Parliament.

But that was only the first step to discovering his Purpose. He had confirmation on the Where, but he was still lost on the What. What did God want him to *do* in politics? William Wilberforce began to pray that God would reveal his Purpose in politics.

At the same time Wilberforce began to pray this very dangerous prayer, there was a group called the Quakers. The Quakers were a group of Christians in England that eschewed the traditional denominations to seek God's leading more directly. They believed God had led them to take on the cause of abolition. They were stirring the pot against the slave trade, but they lacked a real leader, a real voice for the abolition movement, so the movement wasn't getting very far.

That soon ended, once Wilberforce prayed that prayer. He recorded his answer in his prayer journal in October of 1785, where he wrote, "God Almighty has set before me two great objects: the suppression of the slave trade and the reformation of manners."

(Incidentally, Wilberforce doesn't mean that God wanted him to reform the appropriate times to say "please" and "thank you." In this case, "manners" meant "morals." Basically, Wilberforce was saying that God wanted him to lead the fight to redefine what was considered moral—which slavery was at the time.)

And thus Wilberforce's Purpose was made clear to him.

We already know that Wilberforce spent twenty years from then fighting and winning the battle against the slave trade, but he didn't stop there. Over the next fifty years of his life, Wilberforce never wavered from his Purpose, never swerved away from those two great objects.

From that moment until his death, Wilberforce either started or helped to fund 69 different societies that targeted almost every social and cultural issue of his day. Societies against the use of child labor, societies to provide medical care for the indigent, the first SPCA, a Bible society, missions societies, a national gallery of art—he took on everything.

And all because he found that most important thing in life: Purpose.

The interesting thing to note, however, is that he found the purpose *right under his nose*. It was where he already was, doing what he'd already been doing. So many people in our culture are on a search for Purpose, but for Wilberforce—and indeed for most of us—our Purpose lies right at our feet. It's the world around us. Our workplace, our neighborhood, our school.

It's everywhere. It's just up to us to engage it.

Purpose on the Mount

In the Sermon on the Mount, Jesus led with this idea of finding your Purpose where you already are. Let's examine the first verses of this tremendous, countercultural teaching:

"God blesses those who are poor and realize their need for him, for the Kingdom of Heaven is theirs.

"God blesses those who mourn, for they will be comforted.

"God blesses those who are humble, for they will inherit the whole earth.

"God blesses those who hunger and thirst for justice, for they will be satisfied. God blesses those who are merciful, for they will be shown mercy.

"God blesses those whose hearts are pure, for they will see God.

"God blesses those who work for peace, for they will be called the children of God.

"God blesses those who are persecuted for doing right, for the Kingdom of Heaven is theirs.

"God blesses you when people mock you and persecute you and lie about you and say all sorts of evil things against you because you are my followers. Be happy about it! Be very glad! For a great reward awaits you in heaven. And remember, the ancient prophets were persecuted in the same way." (Matthew 5:3-12, NLT)

Again, we have Jesus telling us things that don't make sense. Again, he's implying that we are to relish the times when we want to ball up our fists, stamp our feet on the floor, and say, "God, didn't you *hear* me? This isn't *fair*!"

We'll take the blessing when we're humble or merciful, when our hearts are pure or when we work for peace. That makes sense. But what about this notion that we are blessed when we are poor or in mourning, when we're hungry or thirsty, when we're persecuted? Those make little or no sense to our rational minds.

And yet, if Jesus is to be believed, there has to be some sort of rationale here. It has to come together somehow. It must fit.

One thing to notice: Jesus lists a wide variety of states where we can find ourselves throughout our lives. Sometimes we're poor (if not monetarily, perhaps relationally, emotionally, or spiritually). Sometimes we're in mourning (if not for a loved one then for a lost job or opportunity). Sometimes we're having a good day and are feeling particularly merciful. If we're having a *really* good day, we may be working for peace.

And so we see that God's blessing, sometimes in the form of his Purpose, meets us *where we are*.

We tend to tie the concept of Purpose to success, as if being successful was equal to having achieved God's Purpose for your life. But sometimes success comes at a cost. We can start to view the "successful" in life as those who are rich, who are bombastic and forceful, who are maybe willing to cut a corner or two in order to get ahead.

And yet, Jesus is telling us that those character traits aren't going to get us true blessing. They may get us temporary success, but they won't put us on the road to *his* everlasting success.

It's the qualities opposite of those where blessing

lives. Instead of striving to get out of spiritual poverty, we can find that God, like he did for Wilberforce, will meet us where we are. Instead of shutting off our emotions so we don't mourn, we can find that God will meet us at that place of emotional rawness and give us what we need.

Do you see? God will always put your blessing wherever you are in life. As long as you are looking for him, he will be found. Maybe not right away, maybe not in the way you hope to find him. He may not meet your exact expectations, but he will be there. Always.

And that's where you find your Purpose. You find your Purpose, like Wilberforce did, by looking around you and asking God, "What can I do?"

Have you ever been to Disneyland? If so, have you ever noticed how the place is *always* clean? You'd be hard-pressed to find litter anywhere at the park. Is this because Disneyland has an extraordinary janitorial service? Are they putting the seven dwarves to work at night to scrub the place down?

No. Walt Disney had this idea that everyone had to keep the place clean. If you worked there, and you saw trash, you picked it up. You didn't say, "Well, the garbagemen will come get it soon enough." You didn't make it someone else's problem—you made it your own. Even Disney himself put his words into practice, and consequently set into motion a routine that lasts even to this day.

What if we approached our Purpose like that? What if

we looked around us, saw a problem, large or small, and instead of saying, "I sure hope someone does something about that," we say, "*I'm* going to do something about that." What would happen?

What if we exposed ourselves to the opportunity to find Purpose? This is a key point to the Purpose issue. It is somewhat foolish to pray, "God, what is your Purpose for me?" then stand around for the rest of your life waiting to hear from God.

Get out into the world. Head to some uncomfortable turf. Go places you've never gone before. Wilberforce got an inkling of the basics of his Purpose when he heard about the horrors of the Slave Trade, then had it confirmed by other people in his life whom he trusted. If we follow his example, then what would it hurt to take in the world around us, then, when we get an inkling of what we want to do, bounce it off one or two trusted advisors?

God can't speak to you if you're plugging your ears. Well, he can speak, but you won't hear him. Go out into the world around you, put your ear to heaven, and listen.

Purpose in the Real World: Walt

I (Walt) never wanted to be a minister. Full-time ministry was a shaky proposition, but being a pastor was always something I refused to do. I grew up in a strong Christian home, where my father was a Lutheran minister, and all was not well in his life. Because of his career, he encountered a lot of pain and suffering, from church members who didn't agree with the decisions he made (and who let him know they didn't agree—loudly) to the daily grind of caring for a church and all the little things that have nothing to do with ministry. It wore him down, and I made a conscious decision that I would be *anything* but a minister.

I got to college with the intention of declaring a premed major. I wanted to be a doctor—I figured that was the best way to use my life. I could make people better, help them be healthy, and then they could contribute to God's kingdom.

But as I interacted with my friends and associates in college, I noticed that many of them didn't care about God or Jesus, or even church, really. They thought it was boring and irrelevant to their lives.

Since I was going to college away from home, I was on a search for a church community to join up with. I visited a few congregations and, simultaneously with my realization of uninterested friends, I noticed that these congregations and church communities were desperate for renewed life.

One of the main churches in the community had once been a vibrant center of the community, but over time, the economic landscape of the city changed and the community grew in a different direction. This church, which had once been a hub for the population had now been sidelined into inaction.

I carried a vision of that church within me for the rest of my college years. It was an image that stuck with me, the desperation of this church that had once been so vital and had allowed complacency to suck that vitality away from it.

I graduated and immediately began to wonder if I'd made the right decision. I began to ask a dangerous question: "God, what do *you* want me to do?" I'd already decided long ago what *I* wanted to do, but I'd never really considered what God wanted me to do, because that might involve becoming a minister, and I wasn't going to go through all those things my father went through.

But once I opened up the possibility in my heart, once I let go of my own plans and asked God about it, I heard his voice clearly: he wanted me to become a minister. It was a clear call to full-time, fully ordained ministry.

If I was going to listen to and heed this call, I knew I would have to go to seminary. As I checked into different institutions, I had an interesting conversation with one of the school presidents. We talked at length about the call I felt God had placed upon my life, and he gave me wise words that I still hold on to today:

"Walt," he said, "if you can stay away from here, then don't come at all."

I knew in an instant what he meant. If I wasn't completely hungry, totally thirsty for the call, if I wasn't crystal clear in my Purpose, then I had no business taking it on. It was going to be an uphill climb, and I had to have that tangible Purpose to hang on to, or I wouldn't make it.

As you discover your Purpose, you must keep it in front of you. You must hold on to it, as I had to, as Wilberforce had to. The only easy things in this life are the things that aren't worth doing—when you're out to change the world, you're going to have to fight for it. And when you get in the thick of that fight, it's often difficult to remember why you started fighting in the first place.

Which is why it's so important to keep your Purpose in front of you as you carry it out. If you start out doing a task that relates to your Purpose, it's tempting to let the task become a thing unto itself, until you're focusing on the task instead of the reason behind the task. Keeping your Purpose in front of you helps you focus on the *why* instead of the *what*.

But how can you find the energy to carry out your Purpose? How did Wilberforce find it? Yes, his Purpose gave him a direction, but what propelled him along that direction to his destination? That's exactly what we're going to find out.

CHAPTER FOUR:
Passion

After Wilberforce received Pardon and discovered Purpose, he began to articulate his ideas with the third trait of a world-changer: Passion. His Passion drove him to take up the cause of abolition and run farther with it than anyone had ever done before.

Wilberforce's Passion led him to some areas of self-sacrifice. As we mentioned earlier, he was very much concerned with his social status, with climbing the ladder of success all the way to the top. He grew up with a privileged lifestyle, since he was of the wealthy merchant class, but he wasn't nobility, so he had a desire to grab all that society had to offer.

As we said before, Wilberforce was an avid card-player, so much so that he belonged to five different card-playing clubs in London. It was a source of great enjoyment for him, whiling away the hours in friendly competition with some of his fellow social climbers.

However, when Wilberforce really got a sense of his Purpose, he felt like God was telling him he needed to lay his card-playing down—that he needed to focus his Passion elsewhere. Wilberforce's Passion led him to shift his energies from the frivolities of playing cards and climbing the social ladder to the abolition of the slave trade.

So Wilberforce did it. It wasn't so much that playing cards was wrong; giving up cards was a symbolic act, a way for him to say he was leaving his old passions behind to pursue the greater Passion that God had given him.

And once he got involved in the abolition movement, once he accepted that Passion, it absolutely consumed him. His life was completely changed. The more he exposed himself to the opportunity to support abolition, the more passionate he became. His sense of passion grew until it became almost a righteous indignation at the sub-human treatment of these human beings whom God loved and created.

Wilberforce began to see that slavery wasn't just inappropriate—it was *wrong*, and that became the Passion he pursued for the rest of his life. It is powerfully portrayed in the film *Amazing Grace*, this Passion Wilberforce carried around with him at all times, and it's an accurate reflection of the way Wilberforce felt about slavery in general, not just the slave trade.

Wilberforce was so impassioned by the abolition movement that he captivated audiences every time he spoke about it. One of his famous quotes on the subject of slavery is typical of the type of Passion with which he spoke:

"Africa, Africa. Your sufferings have been the theme that has arrested and engages my heart. Your sufferings no tongue can express, no language impart."

Powerful stuff. And this is the type of language he always used when he spoke about abolition. On the floor of Parliament, as Wilberforce would articulate his arguments against the slave trade, the rest of the members of Parliament would sit quietly, hanging on every word. Even his opponents could not help themselves, listening intently to his fervent discourse.

Wilberforce's Passion so consumed him that he literally spent himself to the point of exhaustion, his sickly frame collapsing from the sheer volume of Passion he poured into his cause.

It caused people to take notice. And when people took notice, he began to change the world.

Passion on the Mount

Jesus gave us some powerful images of Passion in just two verses of the Sermon on the Mount.

"You are the salt of the earth. But if the salt loses its saltiness, how can it be made salty again? It is no longer good for anything, except to be thrown out and trampled by men.

"You are the light of the world. A city on a hill cannot be hidden." (Matthew 5:13-14, NLT)

Salt? Light? What do those things have to do with Passion? Just like always, Jesus is inviting us to look between the lines to see what we find.

Both of these things have qualities that go beyond just themselves. Salt isn't just a white rock. Light isn't just a wave of energy. Salt has inherent saltiness within it, but that saltiness is something that can abate and be lost. Light can shine all it wants, but it has to be directed, or it becomes pointless.

If the salt stops being salty, it's worthless to anyone.

If light isn't directed, if it's hidden away, it isn't going to guide anyone when they're in the dark.

The salt's saltiness, the light's prominent display—these are images of Passion. Because when we have Passion, we automatically illuminate and flavor the world around us. We make the world look and taste better.

And if we don't have Passion? If we lose our savor, if we go dim? Then we have no effect whatsoever. We merely add to the blandness and make no change. It isn't enough to be "salt" and "light" to this world—we must be savory, salty salt; we must be bright, directed light.

We must have Passion.

I have some good news for you about Passion: God works in our hearts to give us Passion. We don't have to drum it up on our own; it isn't up to us to muster our own Passion. In Wilberforce's case—and often in our own world—his Purpose and Passion became like two pieces of iron, each working against the other to sharpen the other.

So if you're still stuck on Purpose, if you're still wondering what "two great objects" God has for you to tackle, take a look at your Passion. Is there anything in the world you're passionate about? What in this world would you gladly invest your time and energy in, if you knew that by doing so you would make a difference?

Is it your family? Your spouse? The homeless? The impoverished? Clean water for the world? Prison reconciliation? Grief counseling? Gambling addictions? Illegal sex trafficking? War victims? This list could go on for pages.

Do you have a Passion? Is there something in your life you feel strongly about? Perhaps that is your Purpose. One doesn't necessarily follow the other; the two work in concert both to direct and fuel your life.

And we see Passion at work even in the life of Jesus, which we obviously know from another excellent film, *The Passion of the Christ*. As that film so eloquently demonstrated, Jesus had a singular Passion to purchase our salvation by following his Father's command. It drove him to hold his tongue when being falsely accused. It drove him to withstand a brutal and sadistic beating. It drove him to carry both a heavy piece of wood and his broken, bloody body up a hill. And finally, it drove him to willingly lay down upon that wood and allow further abuse to his body through three long, cruel spikes.

It is the single most important, most impressive, most humbling display of Passion the world has ever known.

Wilberforce's and Jesus' examples teach us that Passion can indeed *change* the world. They proved that we can do more than just interact with the world. We can do more than entertain it or destroy it. We can do more than associate with it politically or intellectually.

We can change it, and actually transform it.

Social justice is a good thing. Acting on the behalf of those who cannot act for themselves is a good thing. But if we do things without God's perspective, without God's Passion, we run the risk of burnout, and we simply improve the world instead of transforming it.

Think of a house. It's dilapidated and ramshackle. Maybe it was soundly constructed once, but time has not been kind. Weather has warped the exterior boards, the foundation is crumbling, the windows are cracked, and the shingles are either missing or curled from overexposure to sunlight.

Now imagine that you decided to paint it. Would you really be doing that house—or the family who lives in it—any favors? Not at all. You'd be temporarily dressing it up, but the problems of that house go so much deeper than what you see with the naked eye.

When we attempt to change the world on our own, without God's Passion driving us, we are attempting a simple improvement project on a house that needs radical transformation from the foundation up.

The world doesn't need improvement—it needs transformation. This is the type of change God wants us to make (or rather, the type of change *he* wants to make *through* us). And when we do this, when we act out of a God-given Passion, we can feel God's pleasure. And it is good.

Passion in the Real World: Bob

I (Bob) never read the Bible as a kid. Or as a teenager. Or as a young adult. I didn't draw a bead on the Bible until I was a junior in college.

I remember trying to read it a couple of times. But, try as I might, I couldn't get past about the fourth chapter of Genesis. All those genealogies and "begats" just didn't push my buttons.

But after that fateful football fight, and then my subsequent Great Change, I couldn't get enough of the Bible. I sat down to read the Gospel of John and was captivated by what I read; I couldn't wait to read the whole thing.

Bible study soon consumed my life. I pored over it so I could determine how this book, written by different people over a period of centuries, fit together so well. It took over my life so completely that I would often cut college classes so I could stay with the Scriptures (not that I recommend any of you school-age readers doing the same!). That's how much I was captivated by the words of God.

One day I was sitting in my dorm room doing my usual study of the Bible when a thought struck me: "Wouldn't it be great if, for the rest of my life, I got to study the Bible?"

But it wasn't just a thought. It was like lightning struck me. I had instantaneously been invested with my life's Passion.

I suddenly saw the simple decision: if I became a minister, I could do just that! And not just study it for myself, but study it and then teach people about what I studied!

Remember how Walt said he was going to be a doctor before God hijacked his career path? Well, I was going to be a lawyer. I was on the road to law school when I was gripped by this desire to study the Bible for the rest of my life.

Fortunately, like William Wilberforce, I had a wise mentor in my life. I mentioned my new Passion to him, and he decided to let me teach for about fifteen minutes or so at our weekly Bible study meetings.

With fear and trembling, I took him up on the offer and began to teach weekly, and—wonder of wonders—people found it helpful. They found my teaching helpful enough that I was soon encouraged to exit my road to law school and change direction to ministry. I graduated from college and took a position as a youth pastor. I kept studying and teaching the Bible. I finally realized that if I wanted to be able to teach accurately, I needed to go to seminary. As I went to seminary, I continued to teach at every opportunity. I finished seminary and became a teaching pastor at a church, a position I held for twenty years, where we had a significant impact on our community.

Looking back, I can see how my Passion not only drove me in my chosen profession, but how it formed well before that lightning-rod moment in my dorm room. God wired me to look for the way things fit together, they way they mesh to create something new. And God used my life experiences to lead me to that moment when he revealed my Passion to me.

My Passion was a culmination of the things I'd experienced up to that point in my life. And if you'll notice, my Passion for God's word pointed me toward my Purpose of becoming a pastor and minister. Passion and Purpose are irrevocably linked to one another. It was the case for me, and it's something we see almost universally. Even in a scary part of Mexico…

Passion in the Real World: Boys' Town

Kelly Greene is an ordinary woman who is an embodiment of God's Purpose and Passion. There's no other way to put it.

As a young woman, Kelly visited a small town in Mexico called Reynosa as part of a short-term summer missions trip. While there, she heard about a small section of Reynosa called Boys' Town, about a half-square mile of land, walled in by concrete, where the Mexican government allows just about anything. It is rampant with crack bars, regular bars, brothels, and all sorts of unimaginable things.

But it is also filled with people. People whom God loves, and for whom Jesus died. While visiting Reynosa, Kelly heard about Boys' Town, inquiring of her hosts what it was. They told her, and she then spoke the fateful words that would change the course of her life: "Why doesn't anyone do anything to reach those people?"

To which her hosts said: "Maybe God wants *you* to do it."

And so Kelly found her Purpose. Her trip ended and she went back home, but the more she thought about that Purpose, the more God stirred a Passion within her to reach the people of Boys' Town, especially the women trapped in a life of prostitution, who felt they had no other options for their lives. She desperately wanted to relay the love of Jesus to them, but she didn't know what to do about it.

So she began to seek counsel from a missionary mentor, and he had some simple advice: "Go." Everywhere she turned, it seemed as if God was confirming her Purpose while simultaneously growing a Passion within her for what he wanted her to do.

It wasn't long before Kelly packed everything she owned into her white Honda Civic to make the long drive to McAllen, Texas, the American city that lies just across the border from Reynosa. She got hooked up with a church and spent the next few months living first in a small trailer home, then an empty apartment, with no companions but Jesus and a small TV that generated more snow than Siberia.

It was a dark time for Kelly. She didn't know how she was going to reach Boys' Town. She didn't have any real allies. She didn't speak Spanish. She didn't have any formal training in ministry.

But she had Passion. And she had Purpose. And most importantly, she had Jesus.

So Kelly began to pray. As often as she could muster the money for the toll to cross the bridge into Mexico, she would go into Reynosa and walk around the walls of Boys' Town, praying. She would pray for the lost people inside. She would pray for God's power to show up in her life. She would pray for direction, that she would be led by God in her next steps.

And she began to see God move. She began to be emboldened to live out her Purpose. God increased her Passion to a degree that propelled her past all the negativity, all the obstacles, all the seemingly intelligent reasons for her to pull up her stakes and go home.

Gradually, Kelly made her presence known within the walls of Boys' Town. She went inside and began to meet the precious women throwing their lives and innocence away because they felt they had no other choice. She didn't preach at them—she simply loved them. She befriended them. She took an interest in their lives, and in the lives of their children.

And her Passion grew greater. She began to get a vision for a cleaned-up Boys' Town. But she knew that wouldn't happen if she still lived in Texas, so she sought—and received—permission from the Mexican government to purchase land adjacent to Boys' Town so she could build a home, a refuge, a place of hope for all those souls trapped within its walls.

She's seen miraculous things happen. People have been healed. Women have been set free. Hard-hearted, tough-as-nails pimps and drug dealers have had face-to-face experiences with God. A man who owns one of the busiest crack bars in Boys' Town told her she could build a 24-hour prayer room inside it.

And it all comes back to her God-given Passion. Things go fairly well for her now, but those dark times, at the beginning, when she began her journey to the redemption of Boys' Town—she only got through those by remembering her Purpose and by stirring up her Passion. And—we'll discuss this one later—lots and lots of Prayer.

But for now, it's time to examine something else Kelly experienced—and the next thing Wilberforce experienced, too—Power.

CHAPTER FIVE:
Power

In addition to being an eloquent speaker, William Wilberforce was also an eloquent writer. And it was at this time in Wilberforce's life that he began to dig into the scriptures to see what God had to say—not just on the matter of slavery, but on life in general.

This digging developed into a deep, personal devotion to Bible study, prayer, and fellowship with other Christian believers. And the more he discovered about God, the more he realized that he couldn't do a thing under his own power. Even if he'd been given the heart of an ox—which he didn't have—he would've been powerless against the financial behemoth that was the British slave trade.

You see, Wilberforce wasn't just leading a moral crusade. He was leading a movement that impacted people's money.

Wilberforce knew there was no way he was going to win on his own.

So Wilberforce drew on God for Power.

Because God had called him to a Purpose so great, so grand, so earth-shattering, so world-changing that it far outweighed Wilberforce's human ability. It forced Wilberforce to depend on God's Power.

And the way he received that Power was by immersing himself in the things of God.

In addition to changing the world for humankind, Wilberforce also changed the theological landscape of his time. This happened through his highly influential (and loquaciously titled) book *A Practical View of the Prevailing Religious System of Professed Christians in the Higher and Middle Classes of This Country Contrasted With Real Christianity*. (Incidentally, the text is so strong and relevant to today that I (Bob) recently paraphrased the book in modern language and released it under the title *Real Christianity*.)

Despite its hefty handle, the book was a landmark volume on the New Testament that really opened up people's understanding of basic theology that we take for granted today, like justification by faith and the role of the Holy Spirit in the Christian faith. Wilberforce explained the meaning of Christ's sacrifice on the cross, and decoded much of the New Testament in a way that made it understandable.

But one of the biggest things he wrote about was the way God gives us Power to accomplish our Purpose. He understood the inherent truth that we, in our own power, are only subject to failure. That we are weak, fallen creatures who are easily tempted, easily manipulated by our spiritual Enemy. He knew that we are all in need of Pardon, and said as much in his writings.

And yet, even though we don't deserve Pardon, Wilberforce strongly asserted that God grants it to us, endowing us with his holiness through grace. And when he does that, when we accept our inability to live life on our own, then we are given enabling Power. It is a transforming type of Power that converts us from ordinary people into extraordinary world-changers.

Wilberforce's book was addressed to a nation where it was considered the cultural norm to be a Christian—back then, it was the "appropriate" thing to do. And because of this, many people were Christians in name only; their faith was just something they did out of habit, not something that was authentic. This was why so many so-called "Christians" not only allowed the slave trade to continue, but actively profited from it as well.

Since so many Christians had lost sight of the real goal—pursuit of Christ—their thought processes had also gone astray, so they were trying to find power in their own personal possessions or status. But it wasn't a lasting Power, it wasn't God's Power.

Honestly, it was selfishness. And Wilberforce encouraged his readers to let go of that selfishness and begin to focus on living a life enriched by the Power only God can provide.

Wilberforce wrote so authoritatively about God's Power because he had firsthand knowledge, as he had experienced—and indeed *continued* to experience—that Power as he stood on the floor of Parliament and lead the fight for the abolition movement.

Power on the Mount

Jesus uses what has become a very famous illustration in Christian circles that perfectly describes the Power Wilberforce had as he carried on his fight. In the seventh chapter of Matthew, Jesus says:

"Anyone who listens to my teaching and follows it is wise, like a person who builds a house on solid rock. Though the rain comes in torrents and the floodwaters rise and the winds beat against that house, it won't collapse because it is built on bedrock. But anyone who hears my teaching and doesn't obey it is foolish, like a person who builds a house on sand. When the rains and floods come and the winds beat against that house, it will collapse with a mighty crash." (Matthew 7:24-27, NLT)

In these very power-filled hundred or so words, Jesus encapsulates the devotional life of William Wilberforce, and indeed many other world-changers that both came before and followed him.

Breaking it down, we see that Jesus talks about two different kinds of people: people who follow his suggestions and people who do their own thing. Even worse, the latter is a set of people who actively ignore Jesus' suggestions, his teaching. They are people who hear what he says, thumb their nose at him, and say, "That's really nice, but I think I have this all figured out, thank you."

There's a lot that goes into building a house, but the key thing, the first thing you do, is make sure you're building it somewhere safe. These days, we pour a concrete foundation, a solid, level piece of rock that matches the footprint of the house exactly. It is the very thing the house needs. In addition to providing a sure anchor in times of inclement weather, the foundation also protects the house from elements that would destroy it from underneath, like mold, rot, or seeping groundwater.

The foundation is, first and foremost, the strength of the house.

You could build the nicest house in the world, a veritable mansion, with the finest gold inlay, imported marble, highly-polished oak veneer, European bathroom fixtures, plush carpeting, vaulted ceilings—all the things that make a home desirable. But if you build that house on a beach, with no foundation, you're only asking for trouble.

The foundation is where the strength of the house lies. The sand lying beneath your mansion is going to shift and swirl, and eventually, when rains fall and begin to seep underneath, that sand is going to move out of the way, and no matter how grand your mansion, it is going to come down.

The second set of people thought they had it figured out. They traded security for a nice view, and they lost it all. Is it any wonder those people are described as "foolish"?

There is no better word for it. When we decide we know better than God what we are to do, we are foolish.

When we shrug off God's offer of Power to do things

in our own strength, we are foolish.

When we snub the Creator of the Universe, who spoke this very Earth into existence, so that we can mutter to ourselves as we toil by the sweat of our brow, we are foolish.

Not that we aren't to put our own effort into our work. We won't change the world by sitting back in our recliners. No. In Jesus' illustration, the two sets of people both still built houses—it's just a matter of what their house was built *upon*.

In our quest to change the world, we will encounter storms. Our figurative houses will be battered by bad weather, more than once. And if we're attempting to change the world in our own Power, we'll feel those storms keenly.

But if we've built our houses on the foundation of God's Power, we'll weather the storms and come out on the other side even more emboldened to continue the Purpose for which we were called.

A pastor colleague once had an extraordinary vision which we would do well to share here. Sitting in his living room, simply spending time in prayer with God, he experienced a supernatural occurrence, something Christians call an eye-open vision.

It was as if a movie was playing itself out, right there in his living room. He saw a wide-spanning horizon, filled with buildings. They were all short buildings, between one and four stories tall. And then he heard God's voice within his heart: "This is not what I intended."

Suddenly, the image flipped, and instead of low buildings covering the horizon, as far as the eye could see, they'd been replaced with skyscrapers. Buildings that stretched upward as high as possible. And once more, he heard God's voice: "This is what I intended."

He knew he was in the midst of something big, so he waited a moment for God to bring further explanation, which came quickly: "I put skyscrapers in the hearts of my people. They want to accomplish great things, and I want them to accomplish those things. But to build a skyscraper, I have to dig a deep foundation, and my people won't let me dig deep. So they have to settle for low buildings."

In Luke's version of the Sermon on the Mount, Jesus actually says that the person who hears God's words and acts on them is "like a man building a house, who dug deep and laid a foundation on the rock" (Luke 6:48, NASB). It is important that, as we seek God's Power, we also give him access to the deepest parts of ourselves. In so doing, we can accomplish much more than we ever dreamed.

Power in the Real World: D.L. Moody

Perhaps you're reading this book, and this chapter on Power has you perplexed. Perhaps you're thinking, "There's no way I could be like that. Wilberforce and people like him are just too great."

Perhaps. Everyone knows who Billy Graham is, but have you ever heard of a man named Dwight L. Moody? Over 100 years ago, Moody was the Billy Graham of his time, a fire-breathing evangelist who operated in the supernatural Power of God. Thousands of people came to Christ because of his ministry. But he didn't start out that way.

D.L. Moody began his evangelistic career as a shoe salesman. He had a Passion to tell people about Jesus, and so he took any and every opportunity he could to speak and deliver evangelistic messages.

And while Moody had Purpose and Passion, he didn't yet have God's Power. He tried to do it on his own, and he didn't see very many people come to Christ as a result. In fact, he once stumbled upon a drunken man on the street who recognized him.

"Hey," said the man, recognition dawning upon his face "I know who you are. You're D.L. Moody." The man flashed a broad, alcohol-fueled smile. "I'm one of your converts."

"Well, you must be one of *my* converts," said Moody, "because you certainly aren't one of *Christ's*." That this man hadn't been transformed by God was a painful example that Moody had been operating in his own Power instead of God's.

Moody's desire for God's Power was evident in an anecdote from his early life. In conversation with one preacher, he heard the minister say, "The world has yet to see what God can do through one man completely surrendered to the Holy Spirit." Moody replied, "I want to be that man!"

Incidents like this were not uncommon, and Moody had many more people in his life that encouraged him to seek the power of the Holy Spirit to make his work more fruitful. His good friend R.A. Torrey once gave a sermon in 1923 called "Why God Used D.L. Moody," and in this famous biography, he chronicled the event in Moody's life that made a shoe salesman one of the most effective evangelists in Christian history:

...One day on his way to England, [Moody] was walking up Wall Street in New York; (Mr. Moody very seldom told this and I almost hesitate to tell it) and in the midst of the bustle and hurry of that city his prayer was answered; the power of God fell upon him as he walked up the street and he had to hurry off to the house of a friend and ask that he might have a room by himself, and in that room he stayed alone for hours; and the Holy Ghost came upon him, filling his soul with such joy that at last he had to ask God to withhold His hand, lest he die on the spot from very joy. He went out from that place with the power of the Holy Ghost upon him, and when he got to London (partly through the prayers of a bedridden saint in Mr. Lessey's church), the power of God wrought through him mightily in North London, and hundreds were added to the churches; and that was what led to his being invited over to the wonderful

campaign that followed in later years.

In that small room, God began to do an extraordinary thing in Moody's heart and life. God's presence descended upon that room in Power, and, as Moody later described it, became so great that he could no longer bear it and began to pray in reverse, "Stay thy hand, Lord."

But it was too late. God had changed him. Moody had stopped trying on his own strength; instead, he built his house on God's foundation. And suddenly, his evangelistic career completely changed. He began to take every opportunity he could to preach, and he began to see thousands of people come to Christ.

Even other ministers saw God's Power working in Moody. Late in his career, a few ministers in Chicago were planning a crusade, and the general push among them was to invite Moody to come preach. At one point, a young minister rose and challenged the group, saying, "D.L. Moody… D.L. Moody… does D.L. Moody have a monopoly on the Holy Spirit?"

The group sat in silence for a moment before an elder pastor rose and said, "No, D.L. Moody does not have a monopoly on the Holy Spirit. But the Holy Spirit has a monopoly on D.L. Moody."

Moody went on to have a vast influence on foreign missions, on the publishing world, and on academics, founding several schools. And he couldn't take credit for any of it. It was only through God's Power, through God's strength, that Moody had the impact he did.

But Moody, like Wilberforce and Billy Graham and countless others, knew he couldn't do everything by himself. They all had God's help, yes, but they also had regular people helping them as well.

CHAPTER SIX:
Partners

At the same time Wilberforce was discovering God's Power, he also discovered a basic truth about changing the world: he couldn't do it alone. He had to have like-minded Partners that aided him in his task.

Any discussion of Wilberforce's legacy has to include mention of the many Partners who surrounded his efforts and contributed efforts of their own to the abolition movement. Early on in his crusade, Wilberforce met a woman named Hannah More, an English writer and philanthropist who contributed her linguistic skills to the cause. Also coming to Wilberforce's aid early on was his cousin Henry Thornton, a Parliamentarian like Wilberforce, but a man of high integrity and principles who was elected to office despite forgoing the standard custom of buying votes. And of course, Wilberforce had his dear friend William Pitt by his side.

Ten years into his fight against slavery, Wilberforce began to feel the weight of his task, and he began to consider throwing in the towel. Despite his tremendous drive and vision, despite his Passion and Purpose, he still had moments of doubt, and this time, the moment was so long and the doubt so great that he felt he wouldn't be able to continue.

And then he met Barbara Ann Spooner in 1797, just

as he was finishing up *A Practical View of the Prevailing Religious System of Professed Christians in the Higher and Middle Classes of This Country Contrasted With Real Christianity.* Two weeks after their initial meeting, Wilberforce proposed marriage, to which Barbara agreed. They were married a month later, or six weeks after they first met.

Such a whirlwind courtship would seem to be a harbinger of disaster, but in the case of the Wilberforces, it was quite the opposite. In fact, the marriage of William and Barbara Wilberforce was so strong, so unshakeable, that historians agree it had an impact on the institution of marriage in England for the next fifty years. They were held as such an example of strength and fidelity that those around them—and around the country—took notice.

The pair ran against the culture of the time that said it was acceptable to demean women or to be unfaithful to your wife. Add to that Barbara's constant exposure—she was very much a public figure in her husband's life. All these things combined so well that their marriage—and the strength of it—became public knowledge. They raised the bar and modeled something for their culture that was rarely seen at the time.

More importantly, Barbara had a tremendous impact on her husband. She was his constant encourager, his staunch ally, and his fiercest friend. She helped him carry the abolition banner for the rest of his life.

Both Henry Thornton and Hannah More lived in an

area outside London called Clapham, and shortly after their marriage, William and Barbara moved there to interact with their fellow abolitionists. And shortly after that, other like-minded Partners began to move to Clapham, until they had an entire abolition-minded community. It became known as the Clapham Sect or the Clapham Circle.

The Clapham Circle also consisted of people like Thomas Clarkson, a man who devoted his life to abolition after winning an essay competition, researching and writing (in Latin) about the legality of slavery. Another highly influential member of the Clapham Circle was Olaudah Equiano (also known as Gustavus Vassa), a former slave who wrote a scathing autobiography about his time in slavery and the poor treatment he received.

Each of these people contributed their time and gifts to the cause. The famous craftsman Josiah Wedgwood even used his gift of art to create a special medallion that became a symbol of abolition at the time. It was a sort of badge that had an image of a slave, surrounded by the words "Am I not a man and a brother?"

The Clapham Circle had as their center of activity a church called Holy Trinity Clapham, which was pastored by a man named John Venn. Venn became the unofficial pastor of the Clapham Circle, and became a key encourager to the entire community.

Each of these people, even working under God's Power, could only accomplish so much by themselves.

Working together, with God's Power, they multiplied their efforts. They merged their individual Purposes and Passions into a collective Purpose and Passion that was far stronger than any one of them could have ever been. They were the embodiment of Ecclesiastes 4:12 (NIV), which says, "Though one may be overpowered, two can defend themselves. A cord of three strands is not quickly broken."

An interesting thing to note about the Clapham Circle, however, is that each member was already an abolitionist when they came to the party. They already had a God-breathed Purpose, they already had God-fueled Passion, they already had God-given Power—but they only had themselves.

And so God brought them together in Clapham and Partnered them with each other. Generally speaking, God's Purposes always involve something bigger than anything we can accomplish by ourselves. We will almost always have to lock arms with other people to see them through to the end. Just like Wilberforce did.

Partners on the Mount

Jesus addresses the topic of Partners late in the Sermon on the Mount, when he offers this caution:

"Beware of false prophets who come disguised as harmless sheep but are really vicious wolves. You can identify them by their fruit, that is, by the way they act. Can you pick grapes from thorn bushes, or figs from thistles? A good tree produces good fruit, and a bad tree produces bad fruit. A good tree can't produce bad fruit, and a bad tree can't produce good fruit. So every tree that does not produce good fruit is chopped down and thrown into the fire. Yes, just as you can identify a tree by its fruit, so you can identify people by their actions." (Matthew 7:15-20, NLT)

In this passage, Jesus is warning us about enemies we might have, or about people who would seek to do us harm or give us bad information about God with the intent of damaging our faith. He lets us know that we can search those people out by seeing how they act, or, as he calls it, "identify them by their fruit."

We have to be on the lookout for the fruit that people bear, so we can make sure to identify the good from the bad. So that when people tell us one thing but do another, we can catch on to their game and not follow them or listen to what they say.

So, with that in mind, doesn't it stand to reason that we can identify *good* people also by the fruit they bear, by the way they act toward us? By the Passion they may have for their Purpose?

Let's take this metaphor literally for a moment. Let's say God has given you a Purpose and a Passion for picking grapes. Your entire life is consumed by grape-picking; you love the feel of them between your fingers; you dream about grapes and taste them in your sleep—you are about nothing but grapes.

If you were to carry out that Purpose and Passion, would you join up with someone who's all about figs? Or thistles? Or thorns? No way! You'd be on the lookout for fellow grape-lovers, or, in this analogy, fellow grape-producers.

You can't find help from someone who produces thistles; you would be unintelligent to seek assistance from a person who resembles a thorn bush.

It's also good to remember that *we* produce fruit, too. We can't just be on the lookout for grape people if we're sprouting thorns, especially considering Christ's warning that "every tree that does not produce good fruit is chopped down and thrown into the fire." That's a strong admonition to check the fruit we're producing; to check our actions and make sure they line up with what we know to be true and good and right.

We must make sure that our actions and the actions of our Partners are primarily produced by our Passion and our Purpose, through God's Power. If we start to get into ourselves, if we start to get too big for our britches, we stop producing good fruit and start producing thorns and thistles.

But where can we find those same fruit-bearing people with whom we need to Partner? Do we have to go on a journey of a thousand miles to uncover someone with the same Passion who will help us accomplish our Purpose? Not at all.

The answer lies around you. Look around. Chances

are, you already have someone in your life, or near to your life, who shares the same Passion. It might be your spouse. It might be one or more of your children. A parent. Your boyfriend or girlfriend. A good friend from childhood. Your pastor. A coworker. Your boss. A teacher or professor. A neighbor.

The internet has made our world smaller than ever. Perhaps someone on the other side of that modem is someone with whom you should Partner.

Look around at your everyday world and see if a Partner or two springs into view.

And on the off-chance you think you don't need a Partner; if you think you're fine on your own, consider this: Jesus found Partners in the world around him, too.

As Jesus began and continued his ministry, he looked into the souls of the people he found and called a few of them to his side. That's how he gathered his twelve disciples. And even at the end of his ministry, when he was going to the cross, he sent his disciples out in pairs to continue preaching the gospel.

No one in the Bible flew solo, and neither should we.

Partners in the Real World: Allison

I (Bob) have to be honest: my wife Allison is one of my heroes.

In 1996, I was pastoring a church, doing all that a pastor does, and Allison was an all-around awesome wife, involved in the normal ministry things that a pastor's wife gets involved in.

One Sunday we showed a video in church that changed her life completely. It was a video about persecution that still happens in the world today, about the millions of Christians who still suffer for the name of Jesus. Allison saw the video and began to get an incredible Purpose and Passion in her heart for those people. So she embarked on that dangerous prayer: "God, what can I do about this?"

She also asked this question of various organizations and lawmakers, and couldn't get an answer. Everyone knew persecution was happening; no one knew how a regular person could have an effect on it.

Undaunted, Allison began to investigate various agencies in Washington, D.C. to determine which ones worked in the area of helping persecuted Christians, and eventually decided to fly out to the capital to find out how she, as an individual, could help.

When she got to Washington, she discovered that there were actually many people doing things to help persecuted Christians—they just weren't well-known, so their efforts weren't as effective as they could've been if they had more awareness (and therefore more resources). They needed help spreading the word about their organizations and efforts.

So Allison began to work with them to get their message out. Interestingly, one of the biggest proponents of religious liberty that she connected with was Michael

Horowitz, a Jewish man who became an invaluable Partner, along with some other Partners, and together they created the International Day of Prayer for the Persecuted Church, which still occurs on the second Sunday in November.

Having an annual event like the International Day of Prayer for the Persecuted Church greatly helped raise awareness for the topic of persecution in general and these worthwhile organizations in particular. But, for Allison, being Allison, it wasn't enough.

In the process of finding Partners in Washington, D.C., Allison began to work as an independent consultant to some of these organizations to get help for them. As a result, in 2002, she was invited to go to India with a group of women to investigate a religious massacre that had happened in the Indian state of Gujarat.

While in Gujarat, investigating this massacre, she went to a village where a shocking act of brutality had concluded with nineteen men and women—including a member of the Indian Parliament—being burned alive in a house as a result of religious persecution. Allison stood on the pile of ashes that was once nineteen people and a home, and, looking down, saw a key lying there.

It was the key to the house. And it became a symbol to her of all that she stood for. She came back to America and had it made into a pin that she wore frequently, always remembering when she saw it what it represented. It also became a vehicle that led to many conversations about the persecution happening in India.

God began to use the image of that key to form a new Passion that dovetailed with her current Passion for the persecuted church. Her new Passion began to spread to the oppressed people of India, a group of people called the Dalits.

In India, as a result of the Caste system of social hierarchy, the Dalits are an extremely oppressed people. They are considered "untouchable" for no reason other than being born Dalit. They are told from birth that they are lower than human—that they are no better than animals and are therefore only qualified to do menial labor. They aren't educated, they are held in virtual bondage, and they have no sense of self-worth. They don't even know they are worth fighting for.

And there are nearly 300 million of them.

And they've been oppressed for 3000 years.

By the year 2020, one out of every four people on the planet will live in India, making the issue of the Dalits the largest human rights issue in history. It is an enormous task, but Allison has many Partners in her fight to bring the issue of the Dalit treatment to light. She's begun to work with an organization called the Dalit Freedom Network to help these precious, oppressed people. They're building schools for Dalit children. They are telling the Dalits how much they're worth.

More importantly, though, Allison is working in Washington, DC., using some of the same connections she used to instigate the International Day of Prayer for the Persecuted Church, to bring the human rights atrocity of the Dalits to the fore. She's going to every Congressional office and Senatorial office in the capital, as well as to many offices in the White House, to meet with different politicians and talk about what is going on in India.

And as she and her Partners have knocked on doors and had conversations, they've convinced the United States Congress to draft a resolution, making an official statement to the nation of India that America is aware of the situation with the Dalits and that it is completely unacceptable.

This resolution has already passed both the House of Representative Foreign Affairs Committee and was passed on the floor of the House of Representatives. At the time of this writing, it is now in the Foreign Affairs committee of the Senate. And it's all from the work of Allison and the Partners she's surrounded herself with.

It hasn't been easy, by any stretch of the imagination, but Allison has her Purpose and Passion to keep her going, God's Power to extend her efforts far beyond herself, and many like-minded Partners to accomplish her goals, so when the going gets rough, she already has a safety net of encouragement in place.

But there's a crucial element that ties all of these things together, an element that Allison shares with Wilberforce and even Jesus. It's the next character trait of the world-changer: Prayer.

CHAPTER SEVEN:
Prayer

We already established that Wilberforce was intent on studying the Bible (often in the original languages in which the scriptures were written), but his pursuit of God didn't stop with the written word—he also lived a life steeped in Prayer.

Wilberforce believed in the life-altering power of Prayer, that it moves heaven and earth, and his life itself was a magnificent reflection of that belief. In the film *Amazing Grace*, there's a marvelous exchange between Wilberforce and his butler Jeremy, where Wilberforce is asked, "You found God, sir?" and replies, "No, I think God found me." This is the power of Prayer.

Prayer is the act of God getting our attention. It isn't a debate, it isn't an argument—it's the incredible gift of communication with God himself. And Wilberforce recognized the awesomeness of this gift and practiced it daily. He was a man of Prayer.

Wilberforce even mentioned the elemental nature of Prayer to life in *Real Christianity* (also known as *A Practical View of the Prevailing Religious System of Professed Christians in the Higher and Middle Classes in This Country, Contrasted With Real Christianity*, remember?). He believed Prayer was more than a luxury; it was a necessity.

That we should humbly seek God to the extent that we crave a full love for him, until we find ourselves filled to the top with joy, with peace, with hope. He had strong convictions that Prayer (along with Praise) was essential.

He even wrote that negligence in the discipline of Prayer (as well as study of the Bible) would derail us from our Purpose. In his opinion, devotion to Prayer was necessary to accomplishing the tasks set before him—and he felt the same thing applied to anyone who'd accepted Christ's Pardon. He even believed that taking time out of a busy schedule to Pray and study the Bible would create more time in that busy schedule for accomplishing our Purposes. Instead of wasting time we don't have, Prayer gives us extra time we couldn't do without.

Knowing that his country was on a moral and spiritual downward slide, Wilberforce sought out help praying for the nation of England, even in print. He desperately wanted God's help in setting Britain straight on the slave trade issue—and on other issues of morality—so he exhorted his readers to Pray that God intervene in the affairs of the country, even going so far as to chide those who would look down on the practice as pointless, uncivilized, or pagan; for him, it was a given—Prayer was the answer. It was, he points out at the end of his book, the key to starting a lifestyle of changing the world.

Wilberforce trusted *so* much in Prayer that he encouraged his readers to focus intently on Christ, and that

Prayer would then become as involuntary as breathing. This is how much Wilberforce believed in the power of Prayer.

For when Wilberforce Prayed, his focus shifted from himself and from his own career and back to the Purpose and Passion God had placed within him. He prayed that he would be strengthened by God's Power, and he prayed for—and with—his Partners.

In fact, if you were to visit Holy Trinity Church in Clapham, even today, you would find in front of it a table. The table itself is not holy, it is not mystical, it will not heal you if you touch it, it won't turn you into a millionaire. It is a symbol of Prayer.

For around that table, two hundred years ago, the Clapham Circle would gather and Pray for their cause. They would Pray for favor in Parliament. They would Pray for the abolition movement to gain ground. They would Pray for any and every thing they could think of, or that God would put in their hearts.

Because they believed that God chose long ago, from the beginning of time, to be influenced by the Prayers of his people. And even in the midst of difficulty, in the twenty years between the time he began his crusade and the time his first abolition bill passed, Wilberforce and his Partners never forgot that truth. They kept Praying, confident that God would move, sure that God would fulfill their Passion and Purpose in due time.

Prayer on the Mount

The Sermon on the Mount contains the granddaddy of all prayers, the Lord's Prayer. This astonishing model for prayer is beautiful in its simplicity, and it gives us a framework upon which we can base our own prayers. But before he offers the Lord's Prayer, he gives some prayer guidelines:

"When you pray, don't be like the hypocrites who love to pray publicly on street corners and in the synagogues where everyone can see them. I tell you the truth, that is all the reward they will ever get. But when you pray, go away by yourself, shut the door behind you, and pray to your Father in private. Then your Father, who sees everything, will reward you.

"When you pray, don't babble on and on as people of other religions do. They think their prayers are answered merely by repeating their words again and again. Don't be like them, for your Father knows exactly what you need even before you ask him! Pray like this:

"Our Father in heaven, may your name be kept holy. May your Kingdom come soon. May your will be done on earth, as it is in heaven. Give us today the food we need, and forgive us our sins, as we have forgiven those who sin against us. And don't let us yield to temptation, but rescue us from the evil one.

"If you forgive those who sin against you, your heavenly Father will forgive you. But if you refuse to forgive others, your Father will not forgive your sins."

(Matthew 6:5-15, NLT)

There is so much in these mere ten verses that entire books have been written on them. Before we get to the prayer itself, let's examine the structure around the prayer. The ground rules for prayer, if you will. Because those ground rules Jesus establishes around the prayer shows us a key element to prayer: our attitude.

Are we praying loudly and in public so people will see how "holy" we're being? Are we praying with a bunch of words, trying to force God's hand through our eloquence? Are we praying for our own forgiveness while withholding forgiveness from others in our hearts? The Lord's Prayer is bookended by these attitude checks, and we do well when we heed them.

Because, at their root, these attitude checks showcase selfishness. When we pray loudly, we're hoping to be recognized. And, Jesus reminds us, if we get that recognition, that's our reward. And a shabby reward it is.

When we "babble on and on" in our prayers, we're basically saying that, if we just pray long enough, God will hear us. We've put ourselves in charge of God's actions, as if we have to give God an original idea. Not smart.

When we hold in unforgiveness, we tell God that we're better than him. We want him to forgive us while reserving the right *not* to forgive others. Again, we've set ourselves up for a fall onto our own selfishness. And that is only going to lead to frustration.

Now that we've gone over the ground rules, let's look

at Prayer in depth to see what we find.

First, Jesus starts with two simple words that say so much more than just two words: "Our Father." Think of what those words contain. God isn't some distant deity sitting on a high mountaintop; he isn't a disinterested scientist, viewing his little experiment from up above and taking notes to satisfy his own curiosity.

He's our Father. Our Daddy.

It's a position of intimacy, and it hints at a relationship that contains a special bond, the way a loving father loves and cares for his children. A good father spends time with his kids. He encourages them. He embraces them. He reads them bedtime stories. He is irreplaceable.

This is the attitude we need to have toward God. Regardless of the way our earthly fathers treated us, whether they were awesome or abusive or absent, we know the way a relationship with a father *should* be. And that ideal can be achieved through our relationship with God. When we pray, we need to approach him as a loving Father.

After intimacy, we see an attitude of worship, with the words "may your name be kept holy." Since we bear God's name, it is an act of worship on our parts to keep his name holy. To treat him as holy, since he is indeed holy.

By saying, "May your name be kept holy," we are acknowledging God's holiness and his position over us. It is only through his Power that we can do that. And when we acknowledge that holiness, we are worshiping him.

After intimacy and worship, Jesus encourages us to consider relinquishment with the line "May your Kingdom come soon. May your will be done on earth as it is in heaven." It is an attitude of saying that our own will is second place to God's. That, first and foremost, it is *his* will that is to be done, not just in heaven, but here on earth.

By praying that part of the Lord's Prayer, we are saying that we relinquish our own plans, our own designs, our own desires, and giving them up so that God can have his will instead. Again, it is a humble attitude, an issue of our hearts.

Up until now, this model prayer has dealt with God. But the next line of the prayer focuses on daily provision: "Give us today the food we need." God alone is our provider. If we look to anyone or anything else, we can miss out on God's generous provision.

Isn't it great to know that God cares so deeply about us? It goes back to the very beginning of the prayer, when we call him our Daddy. He cares about providing for his children, he cares about making sure that we have what we need, every day.

After providing for us physically, we see that God wants to provide for us spiritually: "Forgive us our sins, as we have forgiven those who sin against us." This line must be important to Jesus, because he emphasizes the point immediately afterward, in the ground rules we've already established.

Forgiveness of our sins is *the* most important thing Jesus provided through his work on the cross. Jesus even remarks on the importance (and seeming difficulty) of forgiveness a few chapters later in Matthew, when some people got upset after Jesus told a paralyzed man that his sins had been forgiven:

"But some teachers of the religious law said to themselves, 'That's blasphemy! Does he think he's God?'

"Jesus knew what they were thinking, so he asked them, 'Why do you have such evil thoughts in your hearts? Is it easier to say 'Your sins are forgiven,' or 'Stand up and walk'? So I will prove to you that the Son of Man has the authority on earth to forgive sins.' Then Jesus turned to the paralyzed man and said, 'Stand up, pick up your mat, and go home!'" (Matthew 9:3-6, NLT)

Jesus was so much more interested in forgiveness that it took precedence over healing. This man was paralyzed, and in Jesus' estimation, he needed forgiveness more than health. Forgiveness is *that* important to God.

After forgiveness, the Lord's Prayer models a prayer for protection: "Don't let us yield to temptation, but rescue us from the evil one." God knows we have an adversary, and he hasn't left us all alone to twist in the wind. We are not alone, unprotected, an easy score for our enemy. We are not Devil-bait.

When we encounter temptation, when we are in the

midst of trials, it's comforting to know that we can pray for strength to withstand it, and for rescue from the traps of the one who would see our downfall.

Though it isn't included in the passage we quoted above, some manuscript copies of Matthew's gospel include a final element to the Lord's Prayer, one which we often quote when reciting it corporately: "For yours is the kingdom and the power and the glory forever. Amen."

This closing statement is a marvelous companion to the opening statement, indicating that the Prayer should begin and end with worship and praise. It is always a very good idea to praise God for who he is and what he's done in our lives.

So there are seven elements to the Lord's Prayer—and indeed to every prayer we should pray: intimacy, worship, relinquishment, provision, forgiveness, protection, and praise. Anything we could ask, think, or imagine, we can fit into this Biblical model of Prayer.

The key thing to remember is that Prayer is a powerful privilege. We don't always immediately see or hear God's answer to our prayers, and he doesn't always answer them the way we want him to. Does that mean we shouldn't pray? Absolutely not! Wilberforce was probably tempted to give up on Prayer at some point during the twenty years he fought the slave trade, but he never did. He kept praying, and God answered those prayers on his own timetable, not Wilberforce's.

Prayer isn't something we can explain. It's just something we practice. Believing, as we do it, that God will hear us and move on our behalf. It is, indeed, our great hope.

Prayer in the Real World: The Dream Center

I (Walt) have a marvelous pastor friend and brother in Christ who can provide us with a perfect example of the power of Prayer.

Tommy Barnett is a pastor in Phoenix, Arizona who felt a Purpose and Passion for the outcasts of his city. The homeless, the prostitutes, the people who were marginalized by society. As he meditated on his Purpose and Passion, he felt like God was giving him Power to reach out to these people through acts of service.

So Tommy and his church members began to go out into the world of these marginalized citizens. They would walk the streets at all hours of the night, just meeting people, talking with them, praying with them, and meeting their practical needs, whether it be food or clothing or something cool to drink.

It was a wonderful start, but it was just that—a start. God had something much bigger in store for Tommy and his son Matt, and that something was called "Los Angeles."

Tommy felt a clear call to extend his Purpose and Passion to the L.A. area, specifically to one of the toughest, hardest sections of the city. Fortunately, Matt shared the same Purpose and Passion, so he became a Partner to his father's ministry and accompanied him to Los Angeles to begin this new endeavor.

As they arrived, they immediately began to seek God in Prayer, asking him to give them direction as the ministry formed. God gave them many more Partners to work with them, and soon they had a thriving ministry to the same people they had reached out to in Phoenix: the homeless, the prostitutes, the people no one cared about.

They began to load up buses at night with people who didn't have anywhere else to go, people who were stuck on the street. Tommy, Matt, and their Partners began to offer more assistance to these outcasts, providing medical care to those who couldn't afford it, and meals to those who were hungry.

Soon, they raised money to purchase an abandoned hospital building in downtown Los Angeles, and they converted it into an all-purpose ministry center, with a large chapel, dormitories, job training facilities, educational services, a large cafeteria, and many other facilities to help them in their Purpose.

The idea was that they could help a person off the street, take them directly to this ministry center, and provide them right then and there with whatever they needed. Housing? Food? Clothing? They had it. If the person didn't have an education, they would be tutored and able to earn a GED. If they had no job skills, they could learn a trade and be able to take care of themselves and their families. If they needed emotional help to break an addiction or a psychological issue, there were counselors available. And if they didn't know Jesus, they had plenty of opportunities to meet him in the regular worship services.

The Barnetts called it The Dream Center.

It was God's dream for Tommy, God's dream for Matt, and God's dream for the city of Los Angeles. If there were people in the city who had no hope for a better life, The Dream Center stood as a testament that it was possible to hope again, to dream again.

But God didn't stop there!

God didn't want The Dream Center to be a place that just drew people; he wanted it to be a place that reached out as well. So the residents and staff of The Dream Center decided to adopt a nearby block.

The block they adopted was one of the most crime-ridden areas of downtown L.A. It was extremely rough, full of drugs and gang violence. To the outside eye, adopting a block like this was a fool's errand. There was no way it could be changed.

Until that block met the power of Prayer.

The Dream Center residents and staff began to walk through the block, meeting with the many people who lived there, talking with them, and—this is crucial—Praying with them. Sometimes, they would just walk through the block and pray without talking to anyone. They would pray as God directed them, praying for various people or addresses.

And the strangest thing happened: this block, the toughest, roughest one in Los Angeles, began to soften. Crime went down. Drug rings were exposed and shut down. Violence decreased.

So they picked another block and did the same thing.

And got the same result.

They're still doing it to this day. And what used to be areas where no one would dare go out at night have become areas of safety and refuge. These extremely terrifying places are now much more peaceful and warm.

And they owe it all to Prayer.

It is a powerful tool in our arsenal as world-changers. Prayer keeps us focused as we go about our world-changing activities, and when all seems lost or when the task looks too difficult, Prayer points us back to God's Power. But it also helps us stay pointed ahead. It helps us exhibit the all-important discipline of Persistence.

CHAPTER EIGHT:
Persistence

In order to see Persistence in Wilberforce's life, we need to back up a bit to the year 1791, when he placed his first bill on the floor of Parliament proposing the abolition of the slave trade. After Wilberforce defended it articulately and eloquently, the bill went up for a vote. And since this chapter is on Persistence, you probably know what happened next: it was crushed, 163-88.

So Wilberforce introduced a bill the following year in 1792. And it was crushed as well.

1793. Crushed. Twice.

1794. Crushed.

You get the picture. He proposed a bill almost every year for seventeen years, and every time he proposed it, it was soundly defeated for one reason or another.

For example, one year, Wilberforce had all the votes he needed for his bill to pass. He'd been meeting with several members of Parliament, and had enough of them convinced to vote against the slave trade that his bill would be voted in by a very narrow margin.

However, as we've already seen, Parliament wasn't exactly packed with men of integrity. Most of the men there had bought their way in, paying off voters to reelect them, so they weren't above manipulating the votes of fellow members of Parliament either.

This particular year, London was hosting a very popular comic opera that was repeatedly sold out. Seeing this show was *the* thing to do in London, and it was extremely difficult to get tickets. Wilberforce's adversaries, on the night of the vote, obtained some of these very hard-to-get tickets and passed them out to his supporters. Those supporters, eager to use their precious tickets, decided to visit the theatre rather than Parliament that night, and Wilberforce's bill was, once again, defeated. Wilberforce nearly had a meltdown from the discouragement.

This type of opposition was indicative of the foes Wilberforce fought, but in addition to resistance from within the Parliament, Wilberforce also encountered opposition from within his own body. There was no way to know it then, but we now know that he suffered from horrible diverticulitis, and was generally a sickly individual. He often was laid up by illness, and sometimes pushed himself to the point of exhaustion or collapse.

But in the midst of all these obstacles, Wilberforce kept submitting the bill, kept his focus on those two "great objects" of his prayer journal, kept his vision on his Purpose and Passion. He kept trusting God's Power, and he and his Partners kept going to God in Prayer. He was 28 years old when he first began his crusade for abolition, and 48 when he saw his bill to banish the slave trade finally pass through Parliament on February 23, 1807.

The world had just changed. And Wilberforce had done it.

And at that moment, as his bill was adopted into law, Wilberforce wept with joy, then turned to his co-conspirator Henry Thornton and said, "Well, Henry, what should we abolish next?"

That is some serious Purpose. That is some unforgettable Passion.

The Clapham Circle, cheered by their victory, carried on in their fight against slavery. Yes, they'd succeeded in getting the slave *trade* abolished, but slavery itself was still legal. People could still own slaves as property, could still treat them essentially however they wanted. They just could no longer buy or sell them.

So Wilberforce's two "great objects" had now been whittled down to one. The slave trade had been suppressed, but now it was time to work on moral reformation. To get people to see slaves as more than property—to see them as humans endowed with, as our own founding fathers put it, inalienable rights.

For the next 25 years, Wilberforce and his Partners in the Clapham Circle fought for the abolition of outright slavery, and encountered the same resistance as before, and had to show the same Persistence as before.

And in 1833, Wilberforce's abolition bill saw the light of day. It entered its third reading, meaning that it was essentially going to be adopted, and three days later, confident that he'd changed the world yet again, Wilberforce died. His bill was adopted into British law a month later, and slavery itself was now illegal.

We owe it all to the Persistence of William Wilberforce, the world-changer.

Persistence on the Mount

Often in scripture, we read words like "endurance," "patience," "steadfast," "persevere," and many other terms synonymous with Persistence. The Bible is packed with instance after instance of rewarded Persistence.

In the Sermon on the Mount, Jesus gives us a couple of those instances of Persistence. The first can be found in the sixth chapter of Matthew:

"Seek the Kingdom of God, above all else, and live righteously, and he will give you everything you need." (Matthew 6:33, NLT)

Interesting that the first word of this verse is "seek," with the understood subject being the word "you." In other words, Jesus is setting us up to be the ones who have to take the first step. It's up to us to do the seeking, to do the righteous living, and then it's up to God to give us what we need. We have to take the lead here.

Have you ever lost your car keys? Or maybe you really want or need to wear a specific pair of shoes, and you can only find one of them. What do you do? Do you shrug your shoulders and say, "Oh well, I can't find my keys; guess I'll have to walk." Do you throw your hands up in the air and say, "Well, I guess this shoe is lost for good; guess I'm going barefoot the rest of my life."

Of course not. You keep seeking until you find what you've lost.

The implication is the same with this scripture. Seeking the Kingdom of God isn't a one-time thing. It isn't something we can do the first time we ever pray, and then sit back, place our hands behind our head, and relax, confident that all our troubles are over. It is a consistent, persistent act that we engage in over and over and over, for the rest of our lives.

Similarly, Jesus expounds on the topic a chapter later:

"Keep on asking, and you will receive what you ask for. Keep on seeking, and you will find. Keep on knocking, and the door will be opened to you. For everyone who asks, receives. Everyone who seeks, finds. And to everyone who knocks, the door will be opened.

"You parents—if your children ask for a loaf of bread, do you give them a stone instead? Or if they ask for a fish, do you give them a snake? Of course not! So if you sinful people know how to give good gifts to your children, how much more will your heavenly Father give good gifts to those who ask him." (Matthew 7:7-11, NLT)

Isn't that good news? Unlike our keys, which just might've found their way into the kitchen trash, or our shoe, which might be buried in the backyard courtesy of the family dog, we're guaranteed when we seek the Kingdom of God. Jesus said so. "Everyone who seeks, finds."

If you seek, you're going to find. Simple as that.

God is not exclusionary. If we keep asking, keep seeking, keep knocking, we can be sure that we'll get an answer, that we'll find what we're looking for, and that we'll be welcomed within. It may not happen *when* we want it to happen, but it will happen, as long as we are persistent.

Look at the analogy Jesus gives after offering his guarantee: he again returns to the image of God as our Father. And a loving Father at that. There's hardly a parent on earth who would be as cruel to their children as the passage suggests, who would give their child a stone if he asked for bread, or a snake if he asked for a fish.

Treating our children well is innate in our nature. And if we, as mistake-prone as we tend to be, can get that right, then doesn't it stand to reason that God, who has never made a mistake, would get it right?

It's interesting that Jesus would use children as a parallel for teaching on Persistence, because, if you have kids, you know how persistent they can be. They are often downright determined, especially when it comes to being fed. If they get their hearts set on a certain snack or, say, pizza for dinner, they let you know. Again and again. Even if they're met with "No" after "No" from you the parent, they'll keep asking until you serve something else. And even then, they might throw a fit about it.

There's something hard-wired within us to be persistent. We recognize it when we're children, and perhaps life beats it out of us as we grow older. But God knew what he was doing when he crafted our guts, and he put that Persistence bone in there on purpose. King David talks about it in one of his psalms:

"You made all the delicate, inner parts of my body and knit me together in my mother's womb. Thank you for making me so wonderfully complex! Your workmanship is marvelous—how well I know it." (Psalm 139:13-14, NLT)

God made us the way he made us for a reason. We are not who we are by chance, as David so poetically described. We are wonderfully complex. We are God's workmanship. We aren't assembled by robotic machines in a people factory somewhere—God took his time with each of us.

And one of the character traits he gave us early on is the trait of Persistence. And then he shows us in the Bible, through the Sermon on the Mount, *why* he gave us that trait—so that it would pay off when we keep asking, keep seeking, keep knocking.

And through that Persistence, we open the door to God's kingdom. Through that Persistence, we see the payoff of all our Purpose and Passion, the workings of God's Power, the fruit of our Partners, and the power of Prayer as it is finally answered.

Persistence is the linchpin of life as a world-changer.

Persistence in the Real World: Desmond Doss

Almost 150 years after Wilberforce lived, during World War II, a man named Desmond Doss became the first conscientious objector to win the Congressional Medal of Honor. His story is a story of unbelievable Persistence, and it resulted in saving the lives of 75 men on an island in the Pacific Theater.

As a Seventh-Day Adventist, Doss would not willingly carry a firearm or willingly kill someone, even if that someone was his enemy. So when he was drafted by the United States military to fight in the war, he marked himself down as a conscientious objector. At the time, most conscientious objectors would either go to work on a farm or in a factory, but since Doss wanted to participate in the battle, he was put on track to become a medic.

Doss's beliefs also forbade him from working on Saturday. It was to be a day of worship, prayer, and study of the Bible. But in boot camp, Doss was not given Saturday off. Until he refused to work.

Because of his stance on his faith, Doss saw intense persecution from his fellow recruits and from his commanding officers, usually in the form of cleaning latrines, while enduring taunts and harassment from his peers. Sometimes worse.

But Doss showed Persistence in his devotion to his faith, and in time began to gain respect for it. He began to win people over, so intense was his Persistence, and so thorough were his medical skills. He was a heroic and skilled medic who showed almost no fear on the battle-field.

Doss's regiment was shipped out to the Pacific and was given what seemed like an impossible mission. They had to help capture a position on an island that would eventually prove to be a strategic position for winning the war: Okinawa. However, there was a catch: they had to approach the island from a side that was comprised of a sheer cliff face, 400 feet high, ending at the top in a flat plateau, upon which were camped opposition forces with their weapons ready to mow down anyone who came up that cliff.

And they were given these orders on a Saturday.

By this time, Doss had so gained the respect of his fellow infantrymen that they refused to go on the mission if Desmond wouldn't go with them. He agreed to go on one condition: that he be allowed to pray and study his Bible that morning. And he was so respected that everyone took him up on it.

After his time with God that morning, they began the mission, and Desmond Doss, conscientious objector, example of Persistence, embarked on astonishing acts of heroism.

Doss's infantry ascended the 400-foot cliff, and as soon as they reached the summit, bullets and mortar shells rained upon them from every direction and from every type of weapon available. When all was said and done, 75 men lay there, injured, exposed to death. And if anyone tried to help them, they risked their own death from enemy fire.

Instead of ducking for cover, Desmond Doss Persisted in his mission both as a medic and a follower of God. Knowing the stakes, he began to retrieve wounded men, one at a time, from the field of battle. He carried them to the cliff edge and lowered them by a rope to his comrades below.

One man after another, after another, after another. 75 times. He saved the lives of every single one of those men.

It would be a great story if it ended there, but it doesn't.

Doss's regiment still had to take the position, so they tried again a few days later, and successfully fought back the enemy. In the process, one of the men went down 200 yards away from him, and, in the face of enemy rifles and mortars blazing away, Doss went after the man and rescued him.

Two days later, he made his way through a volley of grenades, right into the mouth of a cave held by the enemy, to treat the wounds of four fallen men, then transport them to safety, one by one.

The day after that, he helped out an artillery officer who'd fallen, treating the man's wounds, transporting his patient to a safer spot, and delivering plasma to him—all while under enemy fire.

That same day, Doss saw a man injured when bullets

erupted from a cave and ran to the man, a mere handful of yards from the enemy, treated his wounds, and carried him over a hundred yards to a safer position—all while under enemy fire.

And he wasn't done.

Several days later, his company was involved in a night attack, and when it was over, he risked his life administering help to the injured. If he'd been seen by American forces who didn't know he was there, he would've been mistaken for an enemy soldier and, most likely, shot. But he stuck it out, helping those who need help…until a grenade exploded near him and injured his legs.

And he still wasn't done. *Still* he displayed Persistence.

Because if he'd called out for help, he would've endangered whomever came to save him. So he took care of his own wounds and then waited five hours for the sun to rise so he could be transported to safety.

But as he was being transported on a litter (a sort of cot with handles, carried by two other men), they were ambushed by an enemy tank. Another man received wounds that were worse than Doss's, who literally crawled off the litter and demanded that it be used for this other man.

The litter bearers promised to come back for him after they delivered this other man, but as Doss waited for them, he got hit by enemy fire *again*, this time in the arm. Now, in addition to his leg injuries, he had a compound fracture in his arm, which he treated himself by making a splint out of the stock of a rifle. Realizing that he was in bad shape, he then crawled over the rough ground for over 300 yards—that's the length of *three* football fields—to an aid station, and safety.

That is Persistence.

That is going beyond the call of duty.

That is the essence of being a world-changer.

CHAPTER NINE:
What Does It All Mean?

Before we move on, let's take a minute to go over what we've just covered, this time using a modern-day analogy, just for fun.

Changing the world isn't something that can be done in an instant. It's often a lifelong journey, and even when we change one part of it, we aren't necessarily through. As Wilberforce said when his bill to abolish the slave trade was voted in: "What shall we abolish next?"

Thinking along these lines, let's look at our world-changer character traits and compare them to a long-distance road trip. Specifically, we're going to pretend we're a car.

Pardon is the ignition switch on the car. It is the turn of the key that makes movement possible in the first place. If we're going on a long road trip, we won't get far if we have to push the car the entire way. We have to turn the key to get it started, and that's exactly what Pardon does for us.

Purpose is the steering wheel of our lives. It is the thing we use to direct our energy, to point us toward our destination. On our road trip, we use the steering wheel at all times; if we take our hands off the wheel, we're going to get sidetracked by a ditch (or worse). In the same way, we must keep our Purpose in front of us at all times as we seek to change the world.

Passion is the engine of our vehicle. It is the thing that drives us forward. We can have a great steering wheel, but if our engine is broken, we won't be going anywhere. We may be pointed in the right direction, but we have no drive. Passion gives us the drive to keep us going.

Power is the fuel that keeps our engine going. We can have a magnificent, pristine engine that operates flawlessly, but if we don't have fuel feeding it and giving it life, it isn't going to do what it's meant to do. And fuel is something we consistently have to put back into our car—one fuel stop at the beginning of our trip won't cut it. We cannot stop relying on God's Power as we change our world.

Partners are like passengers. Road trips are much less arduous and much more fun when someone goes along with us. They keep us company, help us stay awake when our energy begins to wane, and can even take over at the wheel if we're too exhausted. Yes, we can make it cross-country on our own, but it's much more difficult and isn't nearly as good as sharing the experience with someone.

Prayer is the map, or, for the more technologically advanced, the GPS unit that keeps us on track with our Purpose. If there's a traffic jam ahead, the GPS unit can let you know. If we want to take a scenic route at the last minute, the GPS unit has it immediately figured out. The GPS unit or the map keep us in contact with someone greater than us, someone who sees the whole picture, someone who can tell us exactly where to go. We can only see the road; through Prayer, we get a better idea of the big picture.

Persistence is the cruise control of our car. It is the relentless forward motion that pushes us, mile by mile, toward our destination. Persistence keeps everything on our car working in concert to get us to our destination; it is the dogged determination that sees us through to the end.

Moses the Reluctant World-Changer

By now you've read this book and are probably thinking either one of two things:

1) I can't wait to get started!

2) This is great for someone else, but I can't do it because…

There's always going to be a laundry list of excuses, of reasons you feel you can't do the things God said you can do. Don't worry; you aren't alone. We see this in the Bible, even amongst our greatest heroes of faith.

Can we all agree that Moses was a world-changer? This is the guy who led God's people out of slavery in Egypt and into freedom, and it all started when he encountered the physical presence of God.

Moses was just a plain shepherd, on the run from the law, when he encountered that famous burning bush, a shrub that, though it was on fire, never got any smaller, never turned to ash, never acted like it was on fire. This, in and of itself, would be miraculous. But God took it a step farther and physically spoke to Moses from the bush.

Moses *heard* God's voice. With his ears.

Christians love to talk about hearing God. Even in this book, we've said things like, "I heard God," or, "God spoke to me." But in Exodus chapter three, Moses legitimately hears God speaking to him from the middle of this bush. Even more miraculous, God is calling his name.

"Moses! Moses!" God says.

Wouldn't we be inclined, if we heard the voice of God calling our name from a miracle shrub, to pay attention? To listen numbly and mumble "Uh huh" to everything that God tells us, then dumbly walk around in a daze for a little while?

You know what Moses did? He *argued* with God.

God gave Moses the full story: He has heard the cries of his people, and he is going to send Moses to be their rescuer.

A job! Moses has been given a job—and by God himself, no less. And he was *so* enthused about it, he leapt up and rushed back to Egypt to carry out this monumental task, right?

Not quite. Moses said, "Who am I, that I should go to Pharaoh and bring the Israelites out of Egypt?" (Exodus 3:11, NIV)

God sidesteps the question in the next verse and says, basically, "It doesn't matter, because I will be with you." And then God gives Moses specific instructions on what he's to do, and then, just to encourage him, tells him that the Egyptians are going to give them some parting gifts.

And Moses, hearing this, *then* leapt up and rushed to Egypt. Because who doesn't like parting gifts?

Except he didn't do that. He argued some more. "What if they do not believe me or listen to me and say, 'The LORD did not appear to you?'" (Exodus 4:1, NIV)

At this Moses has crossed the line from "God's servant" to "whiny brat." It is evident that he doesn't want to do this; he wants to go back to his comfortable shepherd's life, and he's hoping that he can throw up enough excuses to get God off his back.

But God, being the determined God that he is, just tells Moses to throw down his staff. It becomes a snake, and God tells him that it's a sign that Moses will give to anyone who questions his authority. Then, just to seal the deal, he turns Moses' hand leprous and back to normal.

So there you go. Moses has the commission, he has

the promise of parting gifts, and now he has some nifty miracles to work. In his mind, he's going through the checklist of excuses, finding that God has already crossed most of them off the list. Ah, but there's one left:

"O Lord, I have never been eloquent, neither in the past nor since you have spoken to your servant. I am slow of speech and tongue." (Exodus 4:10, NIV)

It's just getting pitiful at this point. But God will neither be stumped nor deterred, and tells him, "Look, I made your mouth, Moses. I can give you the speech you need, if that's *really* going to bother you."

Finally, at long last, Moses quits with the excuses and gets to the real issue. "O Lord, please send someone else to do it." (Exodus 4:13, NIV)

He doesn't want to be the guy. He's resisting his destiny to be a world-changer, and we now see that all his excuses have been just that: excuses. They weren't logical, legitimate reasons for him *not* to change the world; they were half-hearted defenses Moses threw up, hoping to block God so he wouldn't have to deal with the real issue—his own heart.

And you know what happened? God got mad. The New International Version of the Bible says "The LORD's anger burned against Moses" (Exodus 4:14, NIV), a feeling Moses most likely understood, what with the burning anger coming from inside a burning bush. God then let Moses take his brother Aaron with him (though one wonders if that wasn't going to be part of the deal anyway).

Moses' excuses weren't enough to deter his destiny—all they did was make God mad.

But I...

Like Moses, we love to offer excuses, especially when God threatens to mess up our comfortable existence of tending sheep all day long. We can come up with all sorts of reasons, go through that mental checklist like Moses did, to avoid doing our part to become world-changers.

Of course, we don't have the benefit of history. We look at that story about Moses and think he looks foolish for being so resistant to God, but only because we know how it ends.

Then we resist the call to become world-changers, but we think we're doing the right thing, because we *don't* know how our own story will end. What if we fail? What if we fall flat on our faces? What if it doesn't work out the way we want it to?

When we offer excuses, we're telling God that we know better. That we can see the end of our story, and we can see that it won't end like Moses' did.

But we're just being short-sighted with those excuses. Because for most of them, God has a response that deflates the excuse and gets back to the issue of the heart. Let's take a look at some of the most common excuses and see if we can offer some encouragement to step into the destiny of becoming a world-changer.

Excuse: I don't have the time. Chances are, you do. A

good practice is to do what some people call a "time budget." Take a week and track the way you spend your time. Physically write it down. After the week, examine your schedule and see if you wasted any time somewhere. You'll likely be surprised. Readjust your time expenditure accordingly.

Excuse: I don't have the money. Changing the world doesn't require an expense account. It doesn't cost a thing to pay a visit to an elderly neighbor. Or to volunteer at a soup kitchen. Or to pick up litter along the highway. Or to pray for your family, your neighborhood, your city, your state, your nation. God wants us to give what we have, and we have many resources other than money.

Excuse: I don't have any talent. You may not be an eloquent speaker (remember Moses?), you may not be able to carry a tune in a bucket, you may not be able to paint even a wall, but you have a gift. God's given us each gifts, and he gave them to us so we can share them with others. Do you like to talk on the phone? Call someone who could use a listening ear. Can you turn your eyelids inside-out? There are probably some parentless kids somewhere who would love to see that. No talent is too small when you put it in God's hands.

Excuse: There's just so much to be done—I can't change everything. No, you can't. But if we all worked together, changing the little things, we could change the world in a day. In the book of Nehemiah, we see that the entire wall around the city of Jerusalem had been destroyed in a war. It was going to be a big job to repair the wall, if one guy did it. But in chapter three, Nehemiah lists all the people who pitched in to help, and even records that "the priests made repairs, each in front of his own house" (Nehemiah 3:28, NIV). By taking small parts of the wall, this large group of people got the job done. Just repair whatever part of the wall is in front of your own house.

Excuse: I'm too old/young. The bottom line is, the Bible is full of people of all ages changing the world. Abraham was beyond his golden years when he had his son Isaac, who would go on to be grandfather to the nation of Israel. David was just a boy when he took down Goliath. If you're drawing breath, you can be a world-changer.

Excuse: I'm afraid I'll mess it up. Fear of failure has paralyzed more than one potential world-changer into inaction. But the Bible comforts us here, in the book of 1 Corinthians. The apostle Paul is talking about converting people to Christianity, and he likens it to a seed: "I planted the seed, Apollos [another apostle] watered it, but God made it grow" (1 Corinthians 3:6, NIV). It's not up to us to achieve results; we're only supposed to plant and water and let *God* do the growing.

Excuse: I have enough problems of my own. It's a funny thing—we can get so consumed with our own problems that we forget the rest of the world has them, too. We lose sight of the opportunities to be a world-changer. But when you begin to do things for others, you'll find that your own problems lose their heaviness. And you'll probably find someone else doing something for you. It certainly couldn't hurt to try.

Excuse: I don't know how. Do you know how to show kindness to someone? Do you know how to smile? Do you know how to deliver groceries to someone who can't get them on their own? Do you know how to unwrap popsicles for the children of a low-rent apartment complex? Do you know how to say nice things about someone? You know how to change the world; you just don't know that you know.

Excuse: I'll get to it tomorrow. If you keep saying this, every day, you'll never get to it. And you aren't always guaranteed tomorrow. The cold hard fact is: there will come a day when you won't have a tomorrow; hopefully you won't wait until then to become a world-changer. Keep your eyes open, keep your ear to the ground, and see if you can't find a way to change a little part of the world *today*.

Excuse: I'm a nobody. What can I do? There are a couple of people other than Moses who tried this one out in the Bible. Gideon, when told by God to save the Israelites from surrounding countries that were bullying them, replied, "How can I save Israel? My clan is the weakest in Manasseh, and I am the least in my family" (Judges 6:15, NIV). Later in history, when God chose Saul to be the first king of Israel, Saul said the same thing: "But am I not a Benjamite, from the smallest tribe of Israel, and is not my clan the least of all the clans of the tribe of Benjamin?" (1

Samuel 9:21, NIV) Of course, both of these men became world-changers. We do everything through God's Power anyway, remember?

Excuse: Someone else will do it. It's a good thing not *everyone* in the world thinks like this, or else nothing would ever get done. It seems that God isn't interested in this excuse, since Moses tried it out on him, and, as we just learned, Gideon and Saul—and none of them got away with it. The point is, God's placed you here on this earth to do something for him, as expressed by the Apostle Paul: "It's in Christ that we find out who we are and what we are living for. Long before we first heard of Christ and got our hopes up, he had his eye on us, had designs on us for glorious living, part of the overall purpose he is working out in everything and everyone" (Ephesians 1:11-12, MSG). You don't get to take a free pass on life.

Excuse: I have physical limitations that will get in my way. So did Wilberforce. It is believed that the Apostle Paul had a physical condition, what he called a "thorn in my flesh" (2 Corinthians 12:7, NIV), that limited him. Joni Eareckson Tada is a quadriplegic who holds a paintbrush in her mouth to create astonishing art. Louis Braille was a blind teenager who invented the braille system of reading at the age of 15. Sometimes the best healing, the best therapy, is to get involved in someone else's life and change their world.

Excuse: The world is fine as it is—it doesn't need changing. If you really offer this as a way to get out of becoming a world-changer, there is little we can do for you. This is the modern equivalent of Moses' pitiful, "O Lord, send someone else." We pray that God would do a work in your heart and open your eyes to see all the transformation around you that needs to occur.

Serve Day

As a final example of world-changing behavior, I (Walt) would like to encourage you with a story about something that happened within my own church.

Several years ago, we decided to do something in our community. We wanted to reach out to the Phoenix area and really get our church congregation involved in the lives of the world immediately around them.

The big dream was to take one day to join together with dozens and dozens of businesses, schools, churches, and multitudes of citizens—locally, nationally, and internationally—to unleash every world-changer around. It was a desire to transform every community—socially, economically, and spiritually.

This desire led us to create an event we called Serve Day. We chose a specific day and organized an effort to get as many members of our congregation involved with going out into our city and performing acts of service. Cleaning up trash along the roadside, visiting the elderly, building a park for homeless children, painting address numbers on curbs so that police and fire departments could locate the houses in an emergency—we did all these types of things and more.

Our congregation caught the vision for Serve Day and anticipation spread like wildfire. When the actual day approached, thousands of people from Community Church of Joy blanketed the greater Phoenix area, taking a mere day out of their lives to contribute a small change of service.

But all those small changes, all those small acts, combined over thousands of people, became a big deal. We had a strong impact on the city of Phoenix and the surrounding area.

We had such an impact that the following year, when we told the city administration that we were planning on doing another Serve Day, we were offered payment. They literally said, "You're doing so much for us that we feel we need to pay you—and we'll still come out ahead."

Of course, we turned them down. World-changers aren't in it for monetary gain; world-changers are in it for the grander reward: spiritual gain.

That year, thousands of people—this time including many from *other* churches—once again went into the city and, combining all their small changes together, made an enormous difference and, to a small degree, changed the entire landscape of the Phoenix area.

Serve Day is now an annual tradition at Community Church of Joy. It isn't about taking one day out of the year to serve the community while withholding the other

364 days for ourselves; Serve Day is a symbol, an annual reminder that one or two small changes, on a big scale, can make a big difference.

And that's what this book is really all about. We hope this book has been a very encouraging motivational movement, like a wise, knowing football coach motivating his players before a big game. We hope you're inspired to go out onto the field and give it your all, to play every down, to leave everything on the field and nothing on the sideline.

Because the moment you close this book, it's kickoff time. The game has begun.

Go play.

FURTHER ENCOURAGEMENT: *More World-Changer Stories*

William Wilberforce is certainly not the only person in the annals of history ever to change the world. He's been our focus over the course of this book, but there are many other people who preceded and followed him who helped alter the course of humanity. And there are people even today doing their part to make this world a better place than the one they were born into.

Below you'll find a glimpse into the lives of a few world-changers. This is not an exhaustive list by any stretch of the imagination; it's merely a few more words of encouragement as you begin your new life as a world-changer. Who knows—perhaps one day *your* name will be on this list.

C.S. Lewis (Early to Mid-Twentieth Century)

Easily one of the most influential Christian minds of the twentieth century, author C.S. Lewis is still having an impact on people today, some forty-plus years after his death.

Lewis wrote many books about the Christian faith, most notably *The Screwtape Letters* and *Mere Christianity*, but his most celebrated work remains *The Chronicles of Narnia*, a magnificent fantasy series that appeals both to adults and children alike. Still, Lewis didn't set out to be a world-changer. In fact, from the age of 13 to the age of 31, he was a devout atheist concerned with his academic career.

It didn't last, though. When he was a teenager, he purchased a copy of the book *Phantastes* by noted Christian fantasy author George MacDonald to read on a train, and the seeds were sown even then for his imminent conversion to Christianity.

Years later, after earning a professorship, he met and became friends with J.R.R. Tolkien (author of *The Lord of the Rings* trilogy) and fellow educator Hugo Dyson. Through these relationships, as well as the book *The Everlasting Man* by G.K. Chesterton, Lewis began to talk through the principles of the faith, and eventually could no longer intellectually and logically argue against the existence of God. He himself said he was dragged kicking and screaming into Christianity, and, in his autobiography *Surprised by Joy*, called himself "the most dejected and reluctant convert in all England."

Still, at this point he had only mentally acknowledged God's existence. It wasn't until two years later, as he rode to the zoo in the sidecar of a motorcycle piloted by his brother Warnie, that he fully accepted Christ. When he began the journey, he had been a theist; when he completed it, he was a Christian.

It is interesting to notice that the life of this world-changer was heavily influenced by so many different people. In this little space alone, we've mentioned George MacDonald, J.R.R. Tolkien, Hugo Dyson, and G.K. Chesterton. Two of them were friends of Lewis, two of them were authors who had no tie to him, yet all four of them were instrumental in changing Lewis's world, who in turn changed ours.

There is no telling how great an impact our small acts of service can have.

Zach Hunter (Present Day)

In William Wilberforce's time, it was estimated that there were 11 million slaves in the world. Today, that estimate is a shocking 27 million. Surely it's a smaller overall percentage of our global population, but it's still a daunting number of oppressed human beings, especially in such enlightened times.

Enter fifteen-year-old Zach Hunter, a regular teenager with a burning Passion to abolish all slavery across the world—for good.

As a normal kid, Zach didn't have the resources to do anything, but he did have a voice, one that he used to start a student-organized fund-raiser called "Loose Change to Loosen Chains." He began his campaign at his high school and raised $6000 in the first two weeks alone. He gave the donations to various abolition organizations and the ball had begun to roll.

Since then, Zach has mobilized thousands of students across the nation to participate in the Loose Change to

Loosen Chains campaign, and has even authored a book entitled *Be the Change* that has become a surprise hit among teenagers, encouraging and inspiring them to become world-changers themselves.

William Wilberforce spent fifty years in his fight against slavery, and he got a late start. With that in mind, there's no telling what kind of things Zach Hunter can accomplish.

Mother Teresa (Mid-to-Late Twentieth Century)

Mother Teresa began life as Agnes Gonxha Bojaxhiu, a humble Albanian, and ended it as one of the most celebrated women of our time. And she's a testament to finding her Purpose simply by looking around her and doing what needed to be done.

As a child, young Agnes was fascinated by stories of missionaries, and, by the age of twelve, had become convinced she was supposed to become one. Six years later, at the age of eighteen, she left home and joined the Sisters of Loreto to devote herself to God and to missions work.

After learning English so she could become a teacher (and renaming herself after the patron saint of missionaries), Mother Teresa moved to India in 1929 and began to teach children in eastern Calcutta, a position she relished.

However, as she looked around her, God began to stir her Passion and her extended Purpose. She was surrounded by so much poverty, famine, and violence that in 1948, she gave in to what she termed "the call within the call" and accepted her Purpose: to help out the poor from within, while living with them.

She would live out this Purpose for the next fifty years, until her death in 1997.

The first year wasn't easy. She had to beg for food and for supplies. She was lonely and full of doubt, but she knew what she was supposed to do, and showed incredible Persistence during the early goings.

Two years later, she started the Missionaries of Charity, which started with 13 care-giving members in Calcutta and today has over 4000 nuns in service around the world, caring for those people no one else will care for.

Mother Teresa believed in a simple world-changing philosophy of looking around her and taking action, as we read in this quote, taken from her book *No Greater Love*: "Love has no other message but its own. Every day we try to live out Christ's love in a very tangible way, in every one of our deeds. If we do any preaching, it is done with deeds, not with words. That is our witness to the gospel."

An Eight-Year-Old Named Emma (Present Day)

At the tender age of five, young Emma heard a clear call from God: she was to be a missionary. She knew within her heart of hearts that God had spoken this call directly to her, and it stirred a Passion for hurting people within her.

Not content to wait until she grew up to start living out that Passion, Emma learned that, through World Vision, she could provide a dairy goat to a deserving third-world family. This family could then use the goat's milk for nourishment for themselves, or, by selling it, for extra income.

Emma loved the idea of meeting practical needs across the world, and, determined to raise the $75 donation, went door to door in her neighborhood explaining her mission. She had the complete donation within less than an hour. She literally changed the world for one family in under sixty minutes.

Since this went so well, Emma then decided to help families in Africa fight malaria. But instead of going door to door, she did something different this time. Enlisting her five-year-old brother and three-year-old sister, Emma secured a large stack of paper, got out paints and paintbrushes, and then proceeded, with her siblings, to paint a ream of pictures. They painted landscapes, animals, their favorite cartoon characters—anything they could think of.

The young trio then brought their newly painted pictures to her father's workplace and went office to office, selling them for whatever people would pay. Emma raised enough money to provide five families with mosquito nets to keep them safe from malaria-infested bites in the middle of the night, and her brother and sister raised enough money to contribute to clean water in villages where such a thing is a luxury.

Additionally, almost all the donors hung up their purchased paintings, which stand as a constant reminder of the need for change in the world. They are still inspired to make a difference in their own worlds because of the difference Emma, her brother, and sister made.

It's also important to note that Emma's parents are as flabbergasted by her behavior as you probably are. They did not point her in this direction, they did not make suggestions—Emma was affected and came up with these ideas on her own. Time will tell, but Emma already has plans to open a medical clinic as part of her missionary efforts, and hopes her brother follows through on his ambition to become a veterinarian so she can recruit him to keep village animals healthy. She is well on the road to being an immense world-changer.

Count Nikolaus Ludwig von Zinzendorf (Early Eighteenth Century)

This German man with an extremely long name is widely considered the first modern missionary, and his teaching, in conjunction with God's Power, spawned a non-stop, continuous prayer movement that lasted for an entire *century*.

As a child, Zinzendorf was exposed to the gospel and developed a deep faith that, like Wilberforce's, challenged his Purpose. Born into wealth and nobility, Zinzendorf was expected to be a Count, but in his heart, he wanted to serve his Savior in full-time ministry. Still, he went through his rigorous education, along the way forming a secret society of adolescent peers called "The Order of the Grain of the Mustard Seed." Order members were committed to using whatever position they attained for God's glory.

During a tour of Europe, Zinzendorf visited a museum and beheld a painting of the crucified Christ emblazoned with the words "This I did for you; what will you do for me?" That sealed the deal, and Zinzendorf, moved beyond words, dedicated himself then and there to his Purpose and Passion: serving Christ.

Assuming his role as Count, Zinzendorf also studied the Bible intently. Soon, a group of Moravians requested permission to live on his land, which he granted. (The Moravians were a sect of Christianity located in what is now the Czech Republic.) The Moravians were troubled with all sorts of in-fighting and division, and, intrigued by them, Zinzendorf began to lead them in daily Bible studies.

A fire of renewal swept through this modest Moravian community, and in the summer of 1727, they experienced unity they'd never had before. By the end of the summer, some of the Moravians there began to carry the gospel to other parts of the earth, while 24 men and 24 women formed a covenant and a schedule to each pray for an hour, thereby creating a complete 24-hour prayer cycle.

It lasted for 100 years.

Zinzendorf also cared for slaves, some fifty years before Wilberforce, though he was German and Wilberforce British. It began when he met a former slave who'd converted to Christianity; it ended when two of the young Moravians actually sold themselves into slavery in order to preach the gospel to slaves.

By the time Zinzendorf died in 1760, he'd established organized missions work throughout Europe, as far north as Greenland, and as far south as South Africa. In short, he literally changed the world of his day.

Tony (Present Day)

I (Walt) had a problem: my church was growing too fast. We had outgrown our building and needed a new place to build a missions center, a place where we could gather on Sundays and worship.

We found the ideal location, an orange grove situated in the perfect part of Glendale, Arizona. We did our due diligence and discovered the land was owned by a man named Tony.

Tony had a reputation for being one of the most raw and ruthless businessmen in our community. Nevertheless, I approached Tony about purchasing the land for our church.

"Do you have any money?" he said.

"Not yet," I replied. "We'll have to raise it."

Our relationship didn't start well. But it started, and

that was the important part. As I met with Tony, my concern began to be less about obtaining this land and more about seeing Tony's life transformed. I invited him to church to see what he would do.

Tony came once. He stood in the back for a few minutes, then left.

He came back again and stood for a few minutes longer this time.

Tony continued coming to our church, and one Sunday after the service, he approached me with the critical question: "You have to be born again to be a Christian. What does that mean?"

I met Tony for lunch to go over his questions and learned the deeper truth of his heart.

"I'm ashamed of my past," he told me. "I know I've done many terrible things in my life. I'm too bad to be able to be forgiven."

I encouraged him that those types of things aren't too bad or too big for God to handle. He accepts us as we are, and there is no sin so great that he cannot forgive it. And there and then, Tony accepted Christ's Pardon.

It transformed Tony's life. Gradually, he became a new man, and everyone could tell it. He began to deal with integrity in his business interests. He became merciful and gracious. He transformed his lifestyle.

And in so doing, he became a world-changer. He changed the lives of his family, of his business associates, through his own life change. He worked with our church to negotiate the purchase of the 140 acres of land where we now reside, and our expanded facilities have allowed us to minister to thousands more people in our area than we had been able to accommodate in our old location.

Tony passed away shortly before our new missions center was complete. A number of years afterward, I ran into Tony's son-in-law at a hotel. We talked briefly about the change in Tony's life, and then he said something that still gives me chills to this day: "My dad's in heaven because of you."

Sometimes the simplest conversations can change someone's world.

Joan of Arc (Early Fifteenth Century)

Here was a woman—a teenager, really—who, like Saul and Gideon, came from humble birth, living in a small village. She was uneducated, could neither read nor write, was untrained in military tactics, and yet Joan of Arc, through God's Power, acted on her Purpose and Passion and changed the nation of France.

At the time of Joan's ascension to popularity, France had been occupied by England for a good hundred years. The monarchy was a mess, there were dual kings involved, illness had run rampant through the land, and the whole place was in need of a miracle.

And that's when Joan made contact with God.

Accounts differ, but Joan was somewhere between

seven and twelve years old when she began to see visions and hear voices, all from departed Saints, all telling her that she was to be the one to end the English occupation of her homeland. Joan had her Purpose, and in her case, her Passion and her Power were the same thing:

God.

At the age of sixteen, Joan sought—and gained—an audience with the king of France, who, surprised at her pluck and wit—and probably tired of losing battle after battle—went out on a limb and granted her request to be placed in command of one of his armies.

And then Joan went on a historic militaristic campaign where she and her army repelled a siege against the city of Orleans in a mere nine days. Months later, she'd commanded battle after battle and greatly squashed the British occupation.

By this time, she was seventeen.

Eventually, Joan was captured, and, in a joke of a trial, convicted of heresy and ordered burnt at the stake. Even so, Joan never denied her God, never denied her beliefs, and never fell into the many logical traps her inquisitors set for her. Sharp of mind and tongue, she skillfully made a mockery of her mock trial.

And when the fateful day of her execution came, she had one request: that she be allowed to look upon a crucifix as she burned. Even in death, her Passion burned brighter than the flames around her.

Though her life was short (she was executed at nineteen), Joan's legacy remains even to this day. Her military devastation was such that the British couldn't remount their army quickly enough, and the war ended some 22 years after her death. She also changed the way the French fought, as they used her aggressive tactics for the remainder of the war. Her name was even lifted up as a symbol of resistance five hundred years later in Nazi-occupied France, during World War II.

That this woman, who spent a scant nineteen years on this earth, could still leave a lasting legacy of inspiration and godliness, is the amazing testament of a woman completely sold on her Purpose and Passion. It is the amazing testament of a world-changer.

Kingdom Assignment (Present Day)

Started by Denny and Leesa Bellesi in Aliso Viejo, California, Kingdom Assignment has inspired hundreds of world-changers throughout the United States and the world.

One Sunday morning, Denny, the pastor of Coast Hills Community Church, asked for one hundred volunteers, people who would like to help God's kingdom. Once he had his volunteers, each of them was handed a crisp $100 bill, with a simple instruction: "Multiply it. Do something extraordinary for God's kingdom."

That simple challenge started a movement.

As the months progressed, world-changing stories began to come in. One person began a ministry to support the homeless. Another woman used the money to support a young single mother with no lifeline; her generosity inspired further generosity, and from that she created a home for mothers in crisis. That home has expanded to a shelter that can house up to five families, and over $1 million has been raised as a result from that single $100 bill, placed into God's hands.

Martin Luther King, Jr. (Mid Twentieth Century)

He had a dream, a dream that we see made manifest today.

He had a dream that changed the world.

As a young pastor in Montgomery, Alabama, Rev. Martin Luther King, Jr. and other Partners leapt to aid a young woman named Rosa Parks who had refused to accept racial discrimination while on a city bus. She was arrested, and, as a public outcry, a boycott of all city buses ensued, a boycott that lasted 382 days.

During this time, Rev. King was arrested, an act that launched him to national prominence. Suddenly, he had a platform for his Passion, and he used it.

He co-founded a group of African-American pastors who intended to use the power of their churches to seek civil rights reform, and through this organization and Rev. King's continued call for nonviolent protest, the issue came to national attention.

It all came to a head in 1963, when King headlined the March on Washington for Jobs and Freedom, a sprawling event attended by some 250,000 people, all packed in front of the Lincoln Memorial, spilling over the National Mall.

Interesting, then, that Rev. King should begin to speak in front of the Lincoln Memorial, a place honoring the man who delivered a very famous speech we call "The Gettysburg Address." Because as Rev. King took the podium, he delivered what would become *another* famous speech: The "I Have a Dream" speech.

The speech was electric. And it did exactly what it needed to do: lay out a case why racial discrimination was wrong, there for the whole world to see. If he wasn't already, he was now the face of civil rights reform in America.

That march and others like it did their job, and the Civil Rights Act of 1964 and the Voting Rights Act of 1965 soon followed them.

Rev. King certainly had many Partners in his efforts, but his Passion and, most assuredly, Prayer, led him to a podium in Washington, D.C., where he had the ear of the world. And then he changed it.

Nelson Mandela (Late Twentieth Century)

As a boy, Nelson Mandela had no real aspirations to anything great; he was a rural kid who was going to herd cattle in his native South Africa. But his father died, and he was sent to live with a rich relative, who eventually was going to hem him in with an arranged marriage. Mandela fled the union, and the rest is history.

Because when he left for the capital city Johannesburg, he became a lawyer, and there experienced firsthand the government-sponsored racism known as apartheid. Blacks were considered non-humans, and things like political power, military opportunity, and basic education were withheld by the mainly white government.

Once he had a taste of outrage, Mandela joined up with programs of passive, nonviolent protest against the policy, programs which were quashed by the government. Eventually, his participation landed him in court, facing what was sure to be a death sentence, when he gave an impassioned statement that catapulted him to national prominence:

"During my lifetime I have dedicated myself to the struggle of the African people. I have fought against white domination, and I have fought against black domination. I have cherished the ideal of a democratic and free society in which all persons live together in harmony and with equal opportunities. It is an ideal which I hope to live for and to achieve. But, if needs be, it is an ideal for which I am prepared to die."

That's some serious Passion. Some serious Purpose.

Mandela sought no legal loophole, but decided to accept his imprisonment as a form of protest and a way to retain his dignity. He turned the prison into an educational facility, christening various instructors to turn the prisoners' free time into a time to learn. His fame began to spread, and Mandela started to change the world from within a prison cell.

Twenty years later, Mandela started working with the government to see his own release from prison—on the condition of ending apartheid and transitioning to a democratic government. And in early 1990, Mandela was released from prison.

Three years later, after winning the approval of his followers and after demonstrating remarkable forgiveness toward those who'd oppressed him personally, Mandela was elected President of South Africa in the country's first democratic election. And his legacy of forgiveness trickled down through the rest of the population, altering the course of his nation. Through his Persistence, he became a world-changer.

BE A WORLD-CHANGER

The Amazing Grace Small Group Bible Study Guide

"IN AN AGE AND COUNTRY FERTILE IN GREAT AND GOOD MEN,
HE WAS AMONG THE FOREMOST OF THOSE WHO FIXED
THE CHARACTER OF THEIR TIMES...."
Westminster Abbey inscription of William Wilberforce

The BE A WORLD-CHANGER Bible Study Guide explores the life, faith, and vision of the great 19th century British reformer, William Wilberforce, as portrayed in the major motion picture *Amazing Grace*.

Wilberforce believed that he and his circle of friends were called by God to pursue two great objects: the abolition of the slave trade, and the reformation of society. The slave trade was the economic and political strength of 19th century Britain – no one dared try to defeat it.

After decades of defeats, Wilberforce's legislation to abolish the slave trade throughout the British Empire became law on March 25, 1807. Along the way, he and his friends launched more than 65 social reforms, including the first animal welfare society, the first Bible society, free education, and laws to protect children and reform prisons.

What would it look like to be a William Wilberforce today? What "great objects" are you most passionate about? What would it take to be a world-changer in your work, church, and neighborhood?

In addition to a comprehensive study on the themes of grace, calling, and perseverance, this five-week BE A WORLD-CHANGER Bible Study Guide gives your small group the opportunity, like Wilberforce, to put your faith into action in a specific "world-changing" community missions project. It is the small acts of service that cause great changes in our homes, our neighborhoods, our churches, our cities, and indeed, our nation and world.

The BE A WORLD-CHANGER Bible Study Guide is best used in conjunction with the major motion picture Amazing Grace. The DVD's Bonus Features contain exclusive scenes that correspond with each week's study. After viewing the entire film, use the questions provided to begin a general discussion about Wilberforce and his remarkable life-story. This will serve as a good introduction to the rest of the study.

The BE A WORLD-CHANGER Bible Study Guide is divided into a four-week study (five weeks with the viewing of Amazing Grace). Each includes opportunities to explore a general theme, to discuss the story, to study the Bible, and to apply the lessons to our lives in a practical way.

The five-week schedule is:

Week One:	*Amazing Grace* Film Night (film is approximately 2 hrs. long)
Week Two:	PARDON, Understanding God's Amazing Grace
Week Three:	PURPOSE, Discovering God's Call
Week Four:	PARTNERS, Pursuing God's Passions Together
Week Five:	PERSEVERANCE, Cultivating Spiritual Disciplines for a Lifestyle of Service

"SERVE DAY": *A Practical Way to Serve Your Community*

At the completion of the BE A WORLD-CHANGER Bible Study Guide, your small group is encouraged to participate in a "Serve Day," a time for concrete acts of service in your community. This could include visiting a nursing home, serving at a Gospel Rescue Mission, cleaning an elderly member's home and yard, or collecting coats and blankets for the homeless. You may want to encourage a church-wide "Serve Day," as a unified and practical way of living out the Gospel in your community.

"Think of ways to encourage one another to outbursts of love and good deeds." Hebrews 10:24 NLT

It was Wilberforce's biblical worldview, his contagious optimism, and his never-ending belief that faith leads to action that set in motion "the great turning point in history," as one historian wrote. In the end, we pray that your study, your conversations, and your service will raise-up a new generation of men and women who, like Wilberforce, change the world through the grace of Jesus Christ.

For more information on the life of William Wilberforce, please visit www.amazinggracemovie.com or review the resources available at the end of the Guide. To let us know how your small group is living out a life of service, like William Wilberforce, please email us at: WorldChanger@amazinggracemovie.com

WEEK ONE: MOVIE NIGHT

Watch *Amazing Grace* as a group, then discuss the following questions:

1. In what ways has this film inspired you? Challenged you?

2. How did Wilberforce's faith motivate his campaign?

3. What role did his friends play in shaping his life and cause? His wife, Barbara? Hannah More? Thomas Clarkson? Equiano? William Pitt? His cousin, Henry Thorton?

4. What lines or scenes particularly stood out to you?

5. What were the central themes of the film?

6. What causes do you care about? Do you have the perseverance, like Wilberforce, to carry-on year after year, defeat after defeat?

7. Why do you think Wilberforce argued that effective social reform should have a spiritual center?

8. Compare the end of Wilberforce's life to the

"retirement mentality" of today?

9. Why might the "reformation of society" be considered an even more challenging task than the "abolition of slavery?"

10. How are the two "objects" related?

11. What are some of the residual effects on our society resulting from the Transatlantic Slave Trade?

12. What are some injustices that are culturally acceptable today?

13. Experts claim that more than 27 million men, women, and children are living in slavery today. Why do you think human trafficking and slavery still exist?

14. What is the biblical response to those living in slavery?

15. What are three practical actions you can take to "reform society"?

16. At the end of his campaign, Lord Fox delivers a moving tribute to Wilberforce. Write a few sentences on how you would like to be remembered at the end of your life.

WEEK TWO: PARDON
– Understanding God's Amazing Grace

"Don't copy the behavior and customs of this world, but let God transform you into a new person by changing the way you think. Then you will learn to know God's will for you, which is good and pleasing and perfect." Romans 12:2, NLT

THEME

The first character trait that made Wilberforce a WORLD-CHANGER is what we will call PARDON. After years as an aimless politician – more concerned about his social status than social causes, Wilberforce experienced what he called a "great change" and became a devoted follower of Jesus Christ.

He witnessed the power of repentance and forgiveness through his spiritual mentor, John Newton, who was a slave-trader turned hymn-writer and pastor. Newton had transported more than 20,000 slaves from Africa to the West Indies. God miraculously intervened in his life and showed him that the grace of Christ is available to even "a wretch like me," a phrase he later included in the lyrics to the timeless hymn, "Amazing Grace."

Jesus said "The time has come, The Kingdom of God is near, repent of your sins and believe the good news!" Mark 1:15 NLT

No matter how far we have strayed or how dark our past, Jesus has promised to forgive our moral failures, our sins, if we ask Him. He said that He will wipe away every sin and remember them no more. This is the ultimate gift of grace – that God, in his mercy, offers us His son, Jesus Christ, so that we can experience an abundant life with God.

The Apostle Paul experienced this life-transforming grace in Christ on a dusty road to the city of Damascus. Read his account in Acts 9:1-20.

SCENE

On the Bonus Features of the *Amazing Grace* DVD, select and play #5 "Once Was Blind."

Wilberforce visits his dear friend and mentor, John Newton, who at the end of his life, and with eyesight fading, is chronicling his years as a slave-trader. It is Newton's "confession." The weight of his life and the glory of God's grace break him. He weeps and tells Wilberforce, "Though my memory is failing, I remember two things very clearly, I am a great sinner and Christ is a great Savior."

FROM THE FILM

1. Compare Wilberforce's first conversation with John Newton to his second. What is different?

2. Newton professes that "I am a great sinner and Christ is a great Savior." How does understanding one's sinfulness deepen one's appreciation of grace?

3. How does Newton acknowledge God's forgiveness? What is his response to Wilberforce at the end of his confession? How does our belief in God's pardon allow us to rise up and do His work without guilt or fear?

FROM THE BIBLE

1. Why does one's sense of guilt vary? Read Romans 1:18b-19, 21, 25, 28 and Judges 21:25.

2. What is the difference between guilt that leads to death and sorrow that leads to life? 2 Corinthians 7:9-10

3. How should guilt be assuaged or remedied? Colossians 21:3-14, Isaiah 53:5-6

4. Earlier in the film, Wilberforce's butler asks, "You found God, sir?" Wilberforce responds,

"I think He found me." What differences are implied about the process of salvation from the perspective of the butler and of Wilberforce? Romans 4:5; 3:24, Ephesians 2:8-9

5. What does it mean to be "found"?

YOUR TURN

1. What is so amazing about grace?
2. Reflect upon a moment that you experienced the power of God's grace.
3. How does your understanding of grace impact your view of forgiveness?
4. What is the difference between confession and repentance? Read Mark 1:15.
5. How can you be an instrument of God's amazing grace?

WEEK THREE: PURPOSE
– Discovering God's Call

THEME

Out of his commitment to Jesus Christ, Wilberforce began to earnestly seek God's purposes for his life. Wilberforce desired to serve God fully – especially in his vocation. He wrestled with whether he should stay in politics or serve as a pastor.

God used Wilberforce's mentor, John Newton, and his friends (the Clapham Circle) to impress upon the young politician that he could "do both," that is, do the work of a politician and the work of God. In his famous diary entry, Wilberforce wrote, "God Almighty has placed before me two great objects: the suppression of the slave trade and the reformation of manners [morals]."

All of us struggle with how to serve God within our vocations. Many of us wonder what "great objects" God is calling us to pursue. We often think that careers in law, medicine, business, and politics are less spiritual or less important than "full time Christian service" in the church or in the mission field. Wilberforce reminds us that God has called each of us to use our gifts and passion for His glory – wherever that might be – as a means of building

His Kingdom in every sphere of society.

"Therefore I, a prisoner for serving the Lord beg you to lead a life worthy of your calling for you have been called by God."Ephesians 4:1, NLT

"For you are God's workmanship, created in Christ Jesus to do good works, which God prepared in advance for us to do." Ephesians 2:10, NIV

SCENE

On the Bonus Features of the *Amazing Grace* DVD, select and play #2 "Clapham Dinner."

After dinner, abolitionist Thomas Clarkson expresses concerns that Wilberforce is having trouble determining whether to "do the work of God or that of a political activist." With a quiet strength and a firm conviction, educator Hannah More appeals, "We humbly suggest that you can do both." Later, Wilberforce's friend, William Pitt, encounters him with the truth that "principles of Christianity lead to action as well as meditation," a direct assault on Wilberforce's temptation to pursue a life of private solitude.

FROM THE FILM

1. Why did Wilberforce view "work of a political

activist" and the "work of God" as separate? How do we reflect the same attitude?

2. How did Wilberforce eventually integrate his faith into his calling as a political leader?

3. Wilberforce was called to "two great objects." He devoted all of his life to this work. The apostle Paul experienced a similar call in Acts 20:24. Does everyone have a "calling"?

FROM THE BIBLE

1. What are some of the purposes or callings reflected in these passages? Read Romans 12:1-8 and I Corinthians 12:1-11.

2. What is the requirement asked of us? Read Micah 6:8, Jeremiah 9:23-24, and Luke 10:27.

3. How should our individual callings incorporate the two most important commandments? Read Mark 12: 30-31.

4. If you do not know your calling, what should you be focused on to help define it? Read 1 John 4:12, 3:23.

YOUR TURN

1. Discuss your hopes for a "Life purpose."

2. What do you think your spiritual gifts might be?

3. Do you have a "great object?" What do you sense is your calling?

4. Have you ever felt conflicted about your vocation in light of what others might consider more "spiritual" occupations?

5. Beyond sharing the Gospel with unbelievers, how can you integrate more of Christ in your vocation, both publicly and privately?

6. How will obedience help reveal and clarify your calling?

PLANNING AHEAD: *"Serve Day" Project*

Now that you have discussed the radical grace of Christ and the call of God in your vocation, pray and discuss how your small group (as well as your church) could be a "world-changer" by organizing a day of service in your community.

Where do you see needs in your church, your community, and/or your country?

A "Serve Day" is a unified effort where you and your small group can make a positive impact on the lives of others by modeling Christ in your community.

Wilberforce believed that small acts of service make a big difference, especially when done with like-minded brothers and sisters. Consider these ideas in helping you decide on what God might be calling you to do together:

- Paint your pastor's and/or staff members' homes or offices.
- Visit nursing home or local hospice and spend time talking with its residents.
- Clean the house or yard of a home bound or ill elderly neighbor.
- Bring blankets and coats to the homeless.
- Deliver meals to your local fire or police department.
- Participate in Angel Tree, a program that delivers toys for children of prisoners.
- Organize a fundraiser for victims of modern day slavery.
- Pick up trash along a major road or at a local park or school.
- Send thank you notes to local military families with spouses, fathers, and mothers serving overseas.

- Participate in a reading program for disadvantaged youth.

WEEK FOUR: PARTNERS
– Pursuing God's Passions Together

THEME

Great pursuits require good friends. Wilberforce surrounded himself with a band of like-minded friends who worked toward "the making of a better world." They were as diverse as they were committed – men and women, believers and unbelievers, educators and businessmen, activists and politicians – all united in a single devotion to righting a great wrong.

When years passed without any visible changes, his friends were there. When enemies rose up against them and defeats threatened to break them down, Wilberforce and his friends held strong. They possessed a patient, persistent vision for change.

Open any newspaper or turn on any news program. It is easy to feel overwhelmed by the weight of the world's challenges. We feel paralyzed to make any substantial difference.

We feel this way because God intended us to live and work in a community. We cannot change the world on our own. A community, united in hope, is able to lift our eyes, steel our will, and rally to our side when all seems hopeless.

Great changes rarely come from a single individual. History is the story of small bands of men and women, who dared to sit, stand, march, fight, defend, pioneer, invent, and even die for the glory of God and the betterment of their fellow man.

Let us think of ways to motivate one another to acts of love and good works. And let us not neglect our meeting together, as some people do, but encourage one another... Hebrews 10:24-25, NLT

SCENE

On the Bonus Features of the *Amazing Grace* DVD, select and play #8 "Our Message was Everywhere."

Wilberforce and his wife, Barbara Spooner, discuss all the actions and events initiated by the Clapham Circle to change hearts and minds in England. Olaudah Equiano signs his best-selling autobiography. Thomas Clarkson rides from town to town, from ship to ship gathering facts and figures on the slave trade, James Ramsey preaches on slavery. It has been said that, "Wilberforce proved a man can change his times, but that he cannot do it alone."

FROM THE FILM

1. Throughout the film we see Wilberforce

in relationships with his cousin, his wife, his political colleagues, and his friends. In particular, how did Wilberforce and Pitt's friendship help them accomplish their respective goals – the end of the slave trade and the rise to Prime Minister?

2. How did the influence of the Clapham Circle shape Wilberforce's calling?
3. Why did the Clapham Circle pursue so many different activities? Why not focus their attention solely on one action?
4. What happened to some members of the Clapham Circle? What brought them back together to finish their work?

FROM THE BIBLE

1. What effect can community achieve that an individual cannot? Read 1 Corinthians 12:12 - 27.
2. What Biblical stories involve partners who together were instrumental in monumental change? Read 1 Samuel 20:42, Numbers 14:30-38, Esther 2:22-28, and Acts 14:3.

3. What was Christ's first priority before he began his preaching ministry? Read Matthew 10:1-4.

4. Jesus assembled a community to serve with Him. The twelve disciples were a diverse bunch of individuals with different personalities, vocations, and strengths. Why didn't Jesus gather people who were all the same? How were they able to change the world? Read Acts 22:15, 4:33.

5. What was distinctive about Jesus' earthly ministry that make relationships one of the most powerful ways to effect change?

YOUR TURN

1. How can friendships inspire courage in those attempting to work for change?

2. Take a few moments in your group to point out the strengths and gifts you see in those around you.

3. What are the positives of being in a community? What are the perceived challenges?

4. Examine your friendships. Do they all look,

act, believe, and live like you do? How do we build authentic friendships with those who are unlike us?

5. Is there a "great object" that you and your friends might pursue together?

PREPARING TO SERVE: *"Serve Day" Project*

By now, hopefully as a group, you have determined the service project that you will take on together.

For the past three weeks, we have been exploring the topics of grace, calling, and community. In light of these themes, we encourage you to assign roles based on

the gifts and talents of each member of your community. For example, some are best serving behind the scenes through the gift of administration. Others are gifted leaders who might take a more public role.

A "Serve Day" checklist:

1. Decide on a day that works for everyone in your small group.

2. Make arrangements with the organization, individual, or ministry where you will be serving.

3. Determine what supplies or resources you will need to complete your service project.

4. Pray that your time will a) help those in need, b) reflect God's love to those you serve, c) bring your small group together in new and meaningful ways, and d) impact your community through the power of the Holy Spirit.

WEEK FIVE: PERSEVERANCE
– Cultivating Spiritual Disciplines for a Lifestyle of Service

THEME

By necessity, Wilberforce learned the lesson of persistence. Nearly every year for seventeen years, Wilberforce's efforts to pass a bill to abolish the slave trade were defeated in the House of Commons. One may wonder what spiritual disciplines would enable a leader to endure defeat after demoralizing defeat – often for reasons attributed to his colleague's laziness or propensity for gambling and theatre rather than legislative duties.

Wilberforce fixed his eyes on something greater than earthly defeats or successes – he looked toward the cross, the best example of victory drawn from suffering.

He also spent years cultivating the spiritual disciplines necessary to work against a great social evil like the slave trade. Temptations, trappings, and temporality stalked him at every turn. Most of the nation was in favor of the slave trade. His body continued to fail him. His defeats made him a mockery in the social classes he once courted. His friends nearly abandoned him.

Among his many accomplishments, Wilberforce was

the first to begin "family devotions" – the daily practice of family prayer and study. He was a student of the Scriptures. His worldview sprang from a deep love of God and His Word, and hour upon hour in prayer.

We tend to overestimate what we can accomplish in a year. We believe if we "just try hard enough," we can accomplish anything. But it is not long before we fudge our strict diet or abandon our gym membership. Eventually we slip into the same old habits – feeling disappointed, defeated, and disillusioned.

It is no wonder that "endurance," "persistence," "patience," and "long-suffering" are not the most popular ideas in our culture today. God, however, calls us to live our lives with a long-term vision, with the knowledge that while we may encounter suffering in this life the prize of salvation awaits us in the next.

"But you, Timothy, are a man of God; so run from all these evil things. Pursue righteousness and a godly life, along with faith, love, perseverance, and gentleness. Fight the good fight for the true faith. Hold tightly to eternal life to which God has called you, which you have confessed before witnesses. And I charge you before God, who gives life to all, and before Christ Jesus, who gave a good testimony before Pontius Pilate, that you obey this command without wavering. Then no one can find fault with you

from now until our Lord Jesus Christ comes again." 1 Timothy 6:11-14 NLT

It doesn't matter whether our life's purpose appears important or not in the eyes of the world, all of us must integrate into our lives the spiritual disciplines modeled by Jesus Christ. (Recommended reading: Richard Foster's *Celebration of Discipline*.) These disciplines include: study of Scripture, prayer, meditation on Christ, reflection on one's life, worship, fellowship with believers, giving of our time and resources, celebration of God's provisions and creation, and solitude.

"Don't you realize that in a race everyone runs, but only one person gets the prize? So run to win! All athletes are disciplined in their training. They do it to win a prize that will fade away, but we do it for an eternal prize. So I run with a purpose in every step. I am not just shadowboxing. I discipline my body like an athlete, training it to do what it should. Otherwise, I fear that after preaching to others I myself might be disqualified." 1 Corinthians 9:24-27 NLT

SCENE

On the Bonus Features of the *Amazing Grace* DVD, select and play #7 "Have You Found God, Sir?"

Wilberforce is sensing a "great change" in his life. Alone

in his manor's garden, he marvels at the delicate design of a spider's web, gazes at the wonders of God's creation, and lies down to converse with God. His butler, Richard, interrupts with the busyness of daily life, leading to a conversation about Wilberforce's new faith and the importance of a well-examined life.

FROM THE FILM

1. What books do you imagine Wilberforce carried with him when he went outside to pray?

2. Wilberforce was a busy man. He was a popular figure at social gatherings, clubs, and parties. Why was it important for Wilberforce to be alone?

3. Why does Wilberforce marvel at the spider's web and the creation around him? What can we learn about ourselves when we gaze upon God's creation?

4. How can Wilberforce's conversation with God instruct our own prayer life?

5. Describe where in this scene we see the disciplines of solitude, celebration, meditation, prayer, fellowship, study, and reflection.

FROM THE BIBLE

1. What does the Apostle Paul recommend that we all do? Read II Timothy 2:15.

2. How is surrender a form of worship? How do you view worship? Read Romans 12:1-2.

3. Why should "The principles of Christianity lead to action as well as to meditation," as seen in an exchange between Wilberforce and Pitt? Read James 2:14-18.

4. How does Jesus teach the disciples to pray? Read Luke 11:1-13.

5. What is the value of perseverance? Read Romans 5:3-4 and James 1:3-4.

YOUR TURN

1. Jesus withdrew from the crowd to pray. When do you take time to withdraw from the crowd?

2. Why do we find it so difficult to cultivate spiritual disciplines?

3. What spiritual disciplines do you most need for your current stage of life? For your work? For your home-life? For your role as parent,

spouse, son/daughter, and/or friend?

4. Jesus says to pray without ceasing. What does He mean?

5. How do spiritual disciplines directly affect one's ability to persevere during trials and defeat?

PUTTING IT ALL INTO PRACTICE: BE A WORLD-CHANGER

"Serve Day" Project

By now, your small group should be ready for your "Serve Day" project. You have assigned tasks and made necessary preparations.

During your time of service we encourage to reflect upon the themes of grace, calling, community, perseverance, and spiritual disciplines.

1. Where were these themes revealed during your day of service?
2. How will you carry-on what you learned in this study and on your day of service?
3. Will you commit to praying that God will reveal to you your "great objects?"

"Pure and lasting religion in the sight of God our father means that we must care for orphans and widows in their troubles, and refuse to let the world corrupt us." James 1:27 NLT

A famous servant to the poor and oppressed encouraged those around her to do "small things with great love." Most of us will never be presidents of companies or personalities on television. Few will direct the course of a nation or give millions away to those in need. But like the Widow's Mite, God calls us to take what we have – our gifts, our resources, and our passions – and direct them toward the service of others. Small things done with great love can indeed change the world.

As the Clapham Circle admonished Wilberforce at that pivotal dinner scene, "If you make the world better in one way you make the world better in every way."

We pray with you that a new generation of Wilberforces – and more importantly of Christ-bearers – will rise up to serve in unimaginable ways for the glory of God and the love of neighbor.

Then you, too, will BE A WORLD-CHANGER.

To share your stories of service and to learn more about Wilberforce, please visit www.amazinggracemovie.com

MORE SMALL-GROUP RESOURCES

Music Inspired by Amazing Grace

Published by EMI-CMG (ASIN: B0000LW7UUK)

Featuring modern day versions of period hymns performed
by today's top Contemporary Christian, Gospel and Country artists.
Smokie Norful
Chris Tomlin
Martina McBride
Marty Stuart with
David Crowder
Kierra "KiKi" Sheard
Jars of Clay
Steven Curtis Chapman with the Wilberforce University Choir

Amazing Grace: William Wilberforce and the Heroic Campaign to End Slavery

by Eric Metaxas
HarperOne (ISBN: 0061173002)

The new biography chronicles British statesman and reformer William Wilberforce's extraordinary contributions to the world, primarily his 20-year fight to abolish the British slave trade. Metaxas re-acquaints

America with this often forgotten moral hero who was an inspiration to Abraham Lincoln and the American anti-slavery movement.

Focus on the Family Radio Theatre®: *Amazing Grace*

Tyndale House/Focus on the Family (ISBN: 9781589973930)

Experience the story of three men whose lives converged at one point in history, changing their world—and ours—forever. From the audio producers who created *The Chronicles of Narnia*® dramas comes Radio Theatre's *Amazing Grace*, an all-new epic. In five hours of drama, listeners will encounter William Wilberforce's early years and the lives of two other reformers. Live the triumph of Olaudah Equiano, a former African slave who bought himself out of slavery and became a best-selling writer. And follow the journey of Captain John Newton—from slave trader, to hymn writer of "Amazing Grace." Brought to life with over 80 voice actors and innovative sound effects, Radio Theatre's *Amazing Grace* presents a fitting prequel to the major motion picture.

go.family.org/AmazingGrace

Visit the website for a FREE download of Olaudah Equiano audio drama

Real Christianity
by William Wilberforce, edited by Bob Beltz
Regal (ISBN: 9780830743117)

From his classic book, *Real Christianity*, William Wilberforce set out to describe for people an authentic expression of the Christian faith, and in doing so, he changed the course of a nation—and the world. With this modern paraphrase of a contemporary classic, Bob Beltz introduces a set of principles critical in living an authentic spiritual life.

Not for Sale: The Return of the Global Slave Trade —and How We Can Fight It
By David Batstone
Harper San Francisco (ISBN: 978-0061206719)

Written by award-winning journalist and professor of ethics David Batstone, *Not for Sale* profiles the new generation of 21st-century abolitionists and their heroic campaign to put an end to human trafficking - while calling readers to action with practical ideas that empower individuals and their communities to join the campaign for human freedom.

Be the Change: Your Guide to Freeing Slaves and Changing the World
by Zach Hunter
Zondervan (ISBN: 0310277566)

Zach Hunter may only be fifteen, but he's taking on issues that affect the world —and he's making a change. Find out how Zach is working to end slavery, and how you can make a difference with the things you see wrong in the world.

Amazing Grace of Freedom
by Ted Baehr, Susan Wales, & Ken Wales
New Leaf Press (ISBN: 9780892216734)

Features an interview with *Amazing Grace* producer, filmmaker Ken Wales. Contains film stills, historic paintings, engravings and documents highlighting a comprehensive collection of essays and commentary from ministry leaders and scholars.

These resources and more are available for purchase at www.amazinggracemovie.com

ADDITIONAL WORLD-CHANGER RESOURCES

Listed below are a few additional resources where you can continue your study on Wilberforce or any of the character traits of a world-changer. We hope you never stop learning in your pursuit to change the world.

William Wilberforce

- *Real Christianity*, William Wilberforce (updated to contemporary language and edited by Bob Beltz), Regal, 2007.
- *Amazing Grace: The Inspirational Stories of William Wilberforce, John Newton, and Olaudah Equiano* (Audio CD), David Arnold and Paul McCusker, Tyndale Entertainment, 2007.
- *Hero for Humanity: A Biography of William Wilberforce*, Kevin Belmonte, NavPress, 2002.
- *William Wilberforce, 1759-1833: A Bibliography*, Leonard Cowie, Greenwood Press, 1992.
- *William Wilberforce*, Robin Furneaux, Regent College Publishing, 2006.

- *God's Politician: William Wilberforce's Struggle to Abolish the Slave Trade and Reform the Morals of a Nation*, Garth Lean, Helmers & Howard, 1987.
- *Recollections of William Wilberforce,* John Hartford, Longman, Green, Longman, Roberts and Green, 1864.
- *Amazing Grace: William Wilberforce and the Heroic Campaign to End Slavery*, Eric Metaxas, Harper San Francisco, 2007.
- *Amazing Grace in the life of William Wilberforce*, John Piper and Jonathan Aitken, Crossway Books, 2007.
- *Wilberforce*, John Pollock, Lion, 2007.
- *William Wilberforce: A Man Who Changed His Times*, The Trinity Forum, 1996.
- *Vital Christianity: The Life and Spirituality of William Wilberforce*, Christian Focus Publications.

Pardon

- *Real Christianity*, William Wilberforce (updated to

contemporary language and edited by Bob Beltz), Regal, 2007.

- *The Ragamuffin Gospel: Good News for the Bedraggled, Beat-Up, and Burnt Out*, Brennan Manning, Multnomah, 2000.
- *The Case for Christ: A Journalist's Personal Investigation of the Evidence for Jesus,* Lee Strobel, Zondervan, 1998.
- *Mere Christianity*, C.S. Lewis, HarperOne (New Edition), 2001.
- *Reign Down: A Call to Personal Repentance*, Walt Kallestad & Shawn Marie Cole, Howard Publishing, being released January 2008.

Purpose

- *The Purpose-Driven Life: What On Earth Am I Here For?*, Rick Warren, Zondervan, 2002
- *The Call: Finding and Fulfilling the Central Purpose of Your Life*, Os Guinness, Thomas Nelson, 2003.

Passion

- *A Passionate Life*, Mike Breen & Walt Kallestad, Cook Communications Ministries, 2005.
- *Be Your Own Creative Coach*, Walt Kallestad, Zondervan, 1998.
- *Talent Is Never Enough: No Matter How Gifted You Are, These 13 Choices Will Make You Better*, John C. Maxwell, Thomas Nelson, 2007.

Power

- *Becoming a Man of the Spirit: A Seven-Week Strategy Based on the Ministry of the Holy Spirit*, Bob Beltz, NavPress, 1999.
- *Entrepreneurial Faith,* Walt Kallestad & Kirbyjon Caldwell (with Paul Sorensen), WaterBrook Press, 2004.
- *Daily Disciplines for the Christian Man*, Bob Beltz, NavPress, 1993.

NavPress, 1993.

- *Becoming a Man of the Word: A Seven-Week Guide to Understanding and Enjoying the Bible,* Bob Beltz, NavPress, 2001.

Partners

- *Life Together: The Classic Exploration of Faith in Community*, Dietrich Bonhoeffer, HarperOne, 1978.
- *The Irresistible Revolution: Living as an Ordinary Radical*, Shane Claiborne, Zondervan, 2006.
- *The Lord of the Ring: In Search of Count Zinzendorf,* Phil Anderson, Regal, 2007.
- *PunkMonk: New Monasticism and the Ancient Art of Breathing*, Andy Freeman & Pete Greig, Regal, 2007.

Prayer

- *Becoming a Man of Prayer: A Seven-Week Strategy Based on the Instructions of Jesus*, Bob Beltz, NavPress, 1996.

- *Letters to Malcolm: Chiefly on Prayer*, C.S. Lewis, Harvest Books, 2004
- *God on Mute: Engaging the Silence of Unanswered Prayer*, Pete Greig, Regal, 2007.

Persistence

- *The Screwtape Letters*, C.S. Lewis, HarperOne (New Edition), 2001.
- *Where Is God When It Hurts?*, Philip Yancey, Zondervan, 2002.
- *My Utmost for His Highest*, Oswald Chambers, Discovery House Publishers, 1992.
- *The Silver Chair*, C.S. Lewis, HarperCollins, 2005.

More World-Changer Information

- For information on learning ethical leadership like William Wilberforce's, visit the Soderquist Center for Leadership & Ethics at www.soderquist.org.
- Learn more about the World-Changers movement